PREPARE
for
BATTLE!

PRAYER IS THE BATTLE CRY OF THE BELIEVER.

For we are not fighting against flesh-and-blood enemies, but against evil rulers and authorities of the unseen world, against mighty powers in this dark world, and against evil spirits in the heavenly places.

—Ephesians 6:12 (New Living Translation, NLT)

PREPARE for BATTLE!

The Battlefield of Spiritual Warfare

Christopher D. Ramey

Copyright ©2023, Christopher D. Ramey

All Rights Reserved. This book may not be reproduced in whole or in part without the written consent of the publisher, except by a reviewer who may quote brief passages in a review. Nor may any part of this book be reproduced, stored in a retrieval system, or transmitted in any form or by any means, electronic, mechanical, photocopying, recording, or other, without the written permission of the publisher.

Hardcover ISBN: 979-8-218-24927-4
Paperback ISBN: 979-8-218-24928-1
E-book ISBN: 979-8-218-24929-8

Cover Design: Style-Matters.com
Cover Imagery: Shutterstock / Nejron Photo

To my wife, Sheryl.

My Sweet Pea. My love. You continue to be one of the greatest blessings God has given me. You love me beyond my faults and see me as a person who is deserving of love. Even though there were times when I didn't think it was possible to find love in this world, God used you to show me what genuine love is. There are no words that I can say that can capture the essence of the love I have for you. I will give you everything that I am for as long as I have breath. I love you, and that will never change, my love. I am proud of who you are, and even more so of who you are becoming.

CONTENTS

Introduction	*ix*
1. Recognizing the Battle	1
2. Prepare for Battle	23
3. Armed for Battle	37
4. Spiritual Warriors	53
5. Never Retreat	71
6. Taking Back Territory	85
7. Facing Your Giants	105
8. The Battle Is the Lord's	119
9. The Blood of the Lamb	131
10. Victory in the Name of Jesus	147
Conclusion	161
Acknowledgments	*165*
About the Author	*173*

The Lord is my light and my salvation—
so why should I be afraid? The Lord
is my fortress, protecting me from
danger, so why should I tremble?

—Psalm 27:1 (NLT)

INTRODUCTION

You are on the battlefield of spiritual warfare. What do you see? What does your battle look like or feel like? Does it feel as if you are in the battle alone? There are times in my walk of faith when I have found myself in a spiritual battle that I felt I would never win. I was victim to the constant barrages of bombs of temptations and the fiery arrows of the enemy. I would feel so overwhelmed in my addiction that I couldn't see past it to recognize the battle that I was in. I would feel so overwhelmed that I would raise the white flag in surrender because I felt as if I was fighting a battle that was unwinnable. I was staring into the depths of the abyss, and there was a fleet of enemies engaging me, ignoring the rules of engagement with the sole purpose of taking me physically and spiritually as a prisoner of war. My enemies were using people far and near—familiar faces and new acquaintances—to trigger my addiction to lust and keep me imprisoned. No matter where I would go, I would have to force myself to look at the floor. I was afraid that a look in the wrong direction would metaphorically be the cell door that would slam shut, the key being thrown away again. I was shackled by lust and imprisoned by something that I saw as inescapable.

I continued to find myself planted in an identity crisis between my flesh and the calling God has for my life. I was trapped within a matrimony between sin and a desire to walk fully into the new creation that I am through Christ. I sought desperately to divorce the connection between who I am and who I used to be. I looked forward to freedom but, was anchored in a time lapse of relapse that would slow down and speed up to replay my mistakes, like a home movie of disgust that was on repeat in the moments of my failures. No matter the direction I chose to navigate my way out of this pit, this dark cloud hovered over me. Meanwhile, the enemy patiently waited for a misstep that could be capitalized to trigger a fall off the mountain of purity and into the valley of sexual impurity. Paralyzed in my spirit, and quickly drowning in shame and guilt, repentance was my safe haven that led back to my Savior and Lord, Jesus Christ. Needless to say, something had to change. I had to change, but I could not be the one who initiated this metamorphosis because I didn't have the power to internally heal and redirect the parts of my life that were unseen to the human eye. A choice had to be made, not from the nucleus of my own strength but as a vertical choice made from my spirit to God—a choice to sever the line of my past that drew me back into my flesh, causing me to drift away from the deep waters of the presence of God. I was a follower of Christ, but I didn't understand why I was still struggling with this sin. I didn't understand the concept of temptation, and because I was a believer, the attacks wouldn't stop. I had to understand the enemy would not stop just because of what God has done in my life. Therefore, I had to learn how to go to battle in prayer.

This journey changed everything for me. I first began to learn that the battle is not mine to fight. I had to take the battle to the master planner, the master strategist, my Father in Heaven. I had to surrender to God all that I was trying to fight on my own strength. I ventured deeper into Scripture and allowed God's truth to penetrate my heart and become the truth that I believed and lived. One of the most powerful passages I have read in the Bible is found in Romans chapter 6. It reads, "For we died and were buried with Christ by baptism. And just as Christ was raised from the dead by the glorious power of the Father, now we also may live new lives. Since we have been united with him in his death, we will also be raised to life as he was. We know that our old sinful selves were crucified with Christ so that sin might lose its power in our lives. We are no longer slaves to sin. For when we died with Christ we were set free from the power of sin. And since we died with Christ, we know we will also live with him. We are sure of this because Christ was raised from the dead, and he will never die again. Death no longer has any power over him. When he died, he died once to break the power of sin. But now that he lives, he lives for the glory of God. So you also should consider yourselves to be dead to the power of sin and alive to God through Christ Jesus" (Romans 6:4–11 [NLT]).

This passage tells me that not only did Jesus die for my sins, but He broke their power over my life before I even knew if, how, or when to put my faith in Him. I was giving power to something that Jesus freed me from when He broke its power over my life. For whomever the Son sets free is free, indeed (John 8:36 [NLT]), and where the Spirit of the Lord is, there is freedom (2 Corinthians 3:17 [NLT]).

Jesus Christ is the key to our chains and the freedom from our oppression.

Jesus Christ is the key to our chains and the freedom from our oppression. He is what frees us from sin and its power. You walk in freedom from the power of sin because of the Lord's Spirit that is within you, and the Holy Spirit makes you more and more like Jesus and less and less like you. This is why you can take the light of Jesus into the darkness, and it will illuminate the darkness and erase it, if you continue to sow seeds of Jesus into the darkness. The chains of addiction had been broken, but it was I who would retreat back to them in an attempt to reconnect what He had already freed me from. When I made the choice to *fully* accept Jesus Christ as Lord by placing my faith in Him, it meant that I would live for Him, and no longer for myself. By living for Him, I would be following His commandments, and not my sinful desires. Following His commandments, His will for my life, and the guidance of the Holy Spirit drew me closer to Him and farther away from sins that my flesh desired daily. This helped me understand how to approach the daily battles that I was facing in prayer. I knew that I had to seek Jesus Christ because it was He who had broken the power of sin over my life, and not me. His blood cleansed and washed me, and I was saved by grace by placing my faith in Jesus for the glory of God.

You cannot march toward the battlefield without Jesus

Christ and His Gospel in your heart. It is the good news that brings the armor of God together. It is the Gospel of Jesus Christ that strengthens you for the battle that is before you. You are never fighting alone, nor have you ever fought alone. God says that He will never leave us nor forsake us. Jesus Christ told the apostles that He would be with us until the end of the age or the world. God is with you, and He will fight the battle for you if you surrender it to Him. God Himself intervened through time in history to come to this earth in the form of flesh to pay a debt that was ours to pay. If God will submit Himself to time because He stands outside of time and is unaffected by time, and intervened to pay the cost of sin, He will also fight your battles for you. One of the descriptive names of God is Jehovah Tsaba, which translates to "the Lord, our warrior." We can find comfort and peace in knowing that the God who created us, loves us, and pursues us will also fight for us. In this life, there will be persecution, hardships, storms, and battles. That is for certain, but the one thing we do know for certain is that God is sovereign and is with us through it all. The epigraph for this book is found in the letter that the apostle Paul wrote to the church in Ephesus. This passage of Scripture is found in chapter 6, and he wrote, "For we are not fighting against flesh-and-blood enemies, but against evil rulers and authorities of the unseen world, against mighty powers in this dark world, and against evil spirits in the heavenly places" (Ephesians 6:12 [NLT]).

The battle that is before you is not one that will be fought under physical circumstances but under spiritual circumstances. Understanding the battle gives you a heightened awareness of how you should approach it. The battle referenced in Ephesians chapter 6 is one fought beyond what the human eye can perceive. I personally believe, in my humble opinion, that most of the battles we face are distractions for bigger attacks. For example, we may be faced with a battle of lust, which can be a distraction for a trap of temptation that leads to adultery—not just within the heart, as Jesus Christ referenced during the Sermon on the Mount in the Gospel of Matthew, but physical adultery. When you persistently lust after the other gender without capturing those rebellious thoughts and making them obedient to Christ (2 Corinthians 10:5 [NLT]), you are leaving the door open for the bigger attack, which could potentially lead to a damaged marriage and divorce. Or, if you struggle with alcoholism, when you are under the influence, it changes your personality for the worse. It fills you with anger, and without dealing with the stress or other things that cause you to seek this medication instead of healing, you could then turn that anger against your family. The battle that is before you may be blinding you to the attack that will flank your blind side. The battle that is before you can take you down, but it is the hit that you do not see that can take you out.

Again, I would argue that the battle that is before you is a distraction from the trap the enemy does not want you to see. It is not the slip or misstep he desires; it is the fall that he seeks. As long as you are focused on what is before you, you will not be vigilant to the things around you. If the battle consumes your vision, the traps that are laid for you will escape your sight. Recondition your vision and shift your focus. Give the battle to God so that He may protect you from the battle you do see and the traps that you do not see. Because only He can protect us from dangers seen and unseen. What the human eye can capture and perceive is limited, but we serve a limitless God who sees all and knows all. It is during my dedicated prayer times that God gives me the strength to press on and endure whatever situation I am currently facing. So I encourage you, when you are standing on the cliff and you are looking down, to seek God in that moment. I would go further to suggest you need to recognize the drift. When you recognize that you are slowly drifting away from God, you need to call upon Him to draw you back to Him. Do not wait until you have fallen down into the valley when you could have called upon the Lord to save you from the fall. He answers and rescues all who call upon His name. He provides a way of escape from all temptation. Do not speed past the escape because the trap is more enticing to you.

For we are not fighting against flesh-and-blood enemies, but against evil rulers and authorities of the unseen world, against mighty powers in this dark world, and against evil spirits in the heavenly places.

—Ephesians 6:12 (NLT)

CHAPTER 1

Recognizing the Battle

Before entering a battle, preparations have to be made. One cannot just go to the front line unprepared; otherwise, defeat will be certain. We cannot allow our hubris to give birth to our demise. The way you approach and prepare for a battle will determine its outcome. However, in order to prepare for the battle, we must first recognize that we are indeed in a battle. Recognizing the battle is the first step of preparation, and this is where we will begin our journey. In order for me to analyze the battles that I have been in, I had to first admit there were areas of my life in which I struggled. Oftentimes, one will allow pride to be at the epicenter of who they are, and because of this, there will be a lack of accountability. If there is no accountability, there will be no honesty. We cannot allow a failure of accountability and honesty to be the weight that causes us to sink into an abyss of sin. Truth sets you free and severs the deadweight that weighs you down. That truth is the Word of God that leads to Jesus Christ—the truth, way, and life. Having no accountability means that you will allow your behavior to go unchecked. What was once something you may have glanced at has now become a thought within your mind. It is a seed that is planted, and it has the potential to take root and grow into your heart if it is not uprooted. What your eyes see, your mind receives, and your heart believes and desires. Because, once it enters your heart, there is potential that it will come out of you in action. If your heart posture is a posture of sin and lust, there is a very high chance your actions will reflect your heart posture. So first, let us recognize the battle within our vision.

The Battle within Our Vision

During my life I have struggled with lust and addictions to pornography and sex. I didn't do myself any favors by allowing my vision to capture glances of lustful images, or simply images of women exercising at the gym. They were there to exercise their stress, distractions, and whatever had clouded their minds throughout the day. They were not there to exercise the lust that was deep within me. That lust had taken root and had grown for more than half of my life. Those women were at the gym for the sole purpose of working out, and not to become a lustful image within my mind. Also, I found myself scrolling social media and viewing enticing images of women. Instead of abandoning this lustful crusade on the seas of Instagram or Facebook, I remained in the depth of it. I was tossed about in the waves of lust and the temptations I had welcomed in, and purity was no longer in my vision. I allowed my eyes to seek things that were not pleasing to God. In the aftermath of my negligent gazing, seeds of lust had been planted within my mind. I felt as if my own eyes were uncontrollable and would wander to wherever they desired; I was unwillingly along for the ride. I had to seek God for the understanding of why I could not control my line of sight or the things that I allowed my gaze to rest upon. Why did it feel as if there was an addiction within my vision to seek lustful things that would do more harm than good? For I did not desire to seek out women who had no relation to me. I did not desire to seek out women who were outside of God's will for me. What I didn't realize was that this was the enemy setting traps around me.

Therefore, I had to learn how to not allow lustful things to capture my vision because, if it captured my vision, it would surely capture my focus. Now I was distracted and unaware of the traps that were set all around me. I had to go into prayer and ask God to give me the strength to not look upon anything that caused me to live a life that was not pleasing to Him. If I could eliminate this step of the battle, there would be no battle within my mind. However, I was not oblivious to the fact that we live in a "less is more" society where the less you wear, the more attention you receive. Society is conditioned to seek out more admiration. Sometimes, this result is revealing flesh to fulfill the space that is void of acceptance within the individual. Maybe the battle they are in is one of the desire to belong and be wanted. To them, *family* is just a word that never manifested within their life. Maybe this is something that has eluded and escaped them for their entire life. They may be children of absent fathers and mothers, who became orphans to the reality of family and were adopted into the ways of the world. It is by no means their fault that my flesh pursued what it desired. That is my fault, and my fault alone. The burdens of my mistakes rest upon me, and me alone. I cannot fault another person for my actions. We are each in a battle; the battlefield, however, may not look the same. The enemy's tactics and the way he will engage warfare is different for each of us. I cannot judge others for the battles that are beneath the surface and blind to the human eye. Because it is hidden so deep within them, behind a mask they wear in public to hide the pain they suffer in private. Regardless of what battle or path you find yourself on, there is a choice. You have a choice to say, *I will no longer allow the void that is within me to control me.* If you recapture your focus, you will recapture your vision.

The more you seek God and go into prayer with honesty and accountability, the more you can begin to progress forward. You have to see beyond yourself to see the God who cares for you and can help you overcome whatever it is that has your vision imprisoned. When you cannot see beyond yourself, you will begin to believe that you are in a battle that is unwinnable. In order to move beyond this, we must condition our vision to see:

- Only things that are pleasing to God
- Only things that He has for you (this is in regard to your spouse)
- That your spouse is more than enough (if you are married)
- That He will provide you with who He intends for you to have (if you are unmarried)

Yes, I know that attraction is not a sin. It is the reaction to the attraction that gives birth to sin. However, if you allow your eyes to continue to be drawn to certain things that are attractive to you, a reaction is imminent. For example, if a glance becomes a gaze, and a gaze becomes a stare, this is progressing beyond simple admiration and attraction. A seed of lust has been sown within your mind, and it is beginning to take root. Now those roots are growing and traveling from your mind and into your heart.

Lust for sexual temptations may not be the weapon your adversary—the enemy—is using against you. It may be lust after various other things such as alcohol, anger, depression, or anxiety. However, there is one thing that I am certain of: if we do not control our vision and allow our sight to go unchecked, we are opening the door for the battle to enter our minds. There is a choice to be made, and this may be a minute-to-minute choice at first, but we have to decide between what we lust after and who we want to become. The choice for me was choosing to look at the floor or in the opposite direction when an attractive woman would walk past me in the gym. This was not due to the fact that I wanted to be impolite or avoid interacting with that person. This was a choice that I made to not allow myself to look lustfully upon another woman who was not my spouse, and to not place myself in a battle. The was a choice to break the cycle. This is how the enemy traps you within sin. He traps you within a cycle, and that cycle is to sin, repent, and repeat. Once you are in this cycle, he will use shame and guilt to keep you trapped. If you are to break free of the cycle, it must begin with a choice. So let the choice you make today be a choice to pursue Jesus with your sight set on Him, and not on the things your flesh craves.

The Battle within Our Minds

If we are unsuccessful at controlling our vision, and we allow our gaze to rest upon things that welcome sin into our minds, we have opened the door for a battle within our minds. I know what it feels like to be under heavy attack within my mind. An endless barrage of invading thoughts had surpassed the protective barriers that were once in place to prevent a free-range attack on my mind. Once the gates have been shattered, and the invaders have infiltrated this space, it destroys your focus and plunders your purity. These invaders imprison your focus and hold you captive under their control. I label these thoughts as invading thoughts because they are unwanted visitors into a place where they are not welcomed. The purpose of invaders is to enter territory and claim it as their own without regard to the present owner or occupant. Your mind is pivotal territory; it is the middle point between your sight and your heart. It is the bridge that allows what you have seen to be formed into a thought that will be transported to your heart. Everything you have done in your life started as a thought or an idea that was formed into a vision to become a reality. Under this premise, what we see becomes a thought or an idea that will lead us to traverse a path that will lead to creating a reality of the thought that had been planted and birthed within our minds. If every thought or idea you are having during this time of your life became a reality, what would be your reality?

Would this be a reality that is centered on the life God has for you? Or would the thoughts you have brought to life be in direct rebellion to the life He created you to live? Just as we cannot allow our sight to go unchecked and gaze upon things that are not pleasing to God, we must also not allow the rebellious thoughts within our minds to go unchecked. We are to take every rebellious thought captive and make it obedient to Jesus Christ. This was penned by the apostle Paul in the book of 2 Corinthians, and it says, "We are human, but we don't wage war as humans do. We use God's mighty weapons, not worldly weapons, to knock down the strongholds of human reasoning and to destroy false arguments. We destroy every proud obstacle that keeps people from knowing God. We capture their rebellious thoughts and teach them to obey Christ" (2 Corinthians 10:3–5 [NLT]). Rebellious thoughts within this context are any thoughts that stem from our sinful nature, human intellect, and anything else that does not promote a life centered on Jesus Christ. Therefore, any thought that is in opposition to a life centered and focused on Jesus is considered rebellious. So now you can begin to recognize the rebellious thoughts that are invading the territory of your mind. You can see the battlefield of your mind being overrun by every rebellious thought that promotes what your flesh craves. There are three things I want to point out within this Scripture:

1. Human reasoning
2. False arguments
3. Proud obstacles

Human reasoning can be simply defined as a thought that is based on evidence and logic. This basically means that a person who is using this sort of reasoning will only believe what they can see and prove by their own understanding and logic. Faith plays no part in this sort of thinking. Sometimes our own logic and reasoning can work against us. For example, if you are going through a tough season in your life, you will begin to believe that God is not with you because you don't see the evidence of His presence. This will paralyze your faith. Our own logic and reasoning without faith can be a fiery arrow in the enemy's quiver to be used against us. Not every thought that is used against us will be an invading thought. Some thoughts will be planted by our own ways of thinking, if we are not anchored in faith. This is a self-inflicted wound within the battle of our minds.

Reasoning and logic without faith fuels the false arguments that we will have within our minds to argue that we are abandoned and alone, when in fact, God is always with us, and He will never forsake us. However, false arguments lead to lies that are hidden behind the fog of truth. A false truth is being masqueraded as truth that now has taken control of not just our minds but our faith as well. These are fallacious ideas that were birthed from rebellious thoughts; they are conceived with the purpose of growing into something that can be used as a barrier to keep us from God, a tool to be used to deeply wound our mental health in the hope of pushing us into depression. We find ourselves in a prison of anxiety, desperately looking for the key to unlock the chains that are wrapped around our minds. In these moments we need not look inwardly but vertically to our Lord and Savior who has the key to free us and break the chains that are wrapped around our minds. So allow the Holy Spirit to lead you out of this self-imposed exile and back to the presence of God.

However, if pride is present, it will hinder the way we approach the escape from this imprisonment. We are blind to the imprisonment, so we must trust in the Holy Spirit to lead us out of it. We do not have the strength to walk away on our own power, but we can be rescued by the power of the Holy Spirit. For a moment, I want you to envision what a prison would look like to you. Would it be an island surrounded by a vast ocean that extends farther than the eye can see? Or would it be a desolate desert with no sign of life? This is what we perceive a wilderness to be. We believe it to be a place of desolation, isolation, and destruction. What led us to the path of this wilderness were the mistakes we may have made. We believe this isolation will soothe the pain that we feel internally. We feel that if we exile ourselves to this place, we won't have to put on a costume while we are in public, a costume to hide who we believe we really are. Some would say that who you are in private is who you really are. This can be a condemning statement for some to hear, and it causes us to go deeper into this exile. What if I were to tell you that God will meet you in the wilderness or prison that you are in and will give you purpose? You may have heard that adversity births purpose. I would say the essence of who we are is sown in the soil of adversity, and how we handled it will determine what grows. Let me give you a few biblical examples.

- **Wilderness:** God met Moses in a self-imposed exile as he was in the wilderness for forty years. Moses left the only place he had ever known as home because he feared for his life. He feared his life would be taken because of the crime he committed by murdering an Egyptian guard to protect a Hebrew (Exodus 2:11–24 ([NLT]).
- **Purpose:** God met Moses on Mount Sinai and called him to be the liberator of his people. Moses went into Egypt and led the children of Israel out of Egypt, just as God had instructed him to do (Exodus 3:1–22 ([NLT]).
- **Wilderness:** Joseph, son of Jacob, was sold into

slavery by his own brothers (Genesis 37:18–36 ([NLT]). He then had an opportunity to serve in the house of Potiphar, but because of the deceit and lies of Potiphar's wife, Joseph was imprisoned (Genesis 39:1–18 ([NLT]).

- **Purpose:** Joseph remained faithful and continued to serve, even during the most troubling times of his life. He was freed from prison due to the fact that he was able to interpret the dreams of the pharaoh (Genesis 41:1–36 ([NLT]). The dream was that a seven-year famine would take place. Joseph was appointed as second in command over all of Egypt (Genesis 41:37–57 ([NLT]). During this time, he stewarded over the resources that Egypt produced. Once the famine came, they were more than prepared to withstand it. They also would provide aid to other nations, including those of the brothers who had sold him into slavery (Genesis 45:1–28 ([NLT]). In the country he had entered as a slave, he became second in command. This was the purpose God had for Joseph in Egypt.

I mention all of this to say that, no matter how deep you think you are buried under your mistakes, something can still grow. Something living can come forth in places that were once barren and desolate.

The Battle within Our Hearts

I will start this section by sharing something that I wrote in the notes section of my iPhone during a very rough day:

> Life and work have been a fog as of late. A monotonous barrier that has me engaged in an identity crisis between my flesh and my purpose in life from God. It is a matrimony between sin and a desire to walk fully into the new creation that I am. A spiritual metamorphosis has taken place, but at times, it feels as if the reverse osmosis that has taken place within me did not remove the impurities within me. A time lapse of relapse that slows down and speeds up within time to replay my mistakes. A home movie of disgust that is on repeat in the moment of my failure. A cloud that hovers as the enemy waits patiently for a misstep that can be capitalized to trigger a fall. I feel as if I am paralyzed in my spirit; quickly drowning

in shame and guilt. Repentance is my safe haven that leads back to my Lord and Savior, Jesus Christ.

The battles within our hearts can take us to very dark places absent of light. What enters your heart has the potential to send you into a spiritual cardiac arrest, taking the very life out of your faith and desire to fight for who you are becoming. This is why the Bible tells us to guard our hearts, because the heart is the very origin of sin and faith (Proverb 4:23 ([NLT]). God wants our hearts, and so does the enemy, because you will pursue your heart's desires. Every action begins with a thought or an idea that travels to the heart. The thought then becomes a desire; and once it becomes a desire, it will transform to action. This is why we cannot allow sin to enter our hearts.

We know about the three foundational sins: the lust of the flesh, the lust of the eyes, and the pride of life. Lust has been my struggle, as you may have figured out by now. When people hear the word lust, in most cases, it is automatically assumed to be sexual in nature. In fact, lust is basically a strong desire or craving for a particular thing. When you lust after something, you crave it. Our sinful nature craves things that are opposite of what the Holy Spirit desires for our lives. When you crave something, there is a powerful compulsion that fuels your pursuit of the thing you crave. There is an internal compulsive force driving you toward it. When you desire something, you strongly wish for it or want it to happen. We follow the Holy Spirit because we desire to live lives that are fruitful and pleasing to God. There is a difference between desiring something and craving something. When you desire something, there is an expression of longing. When you crave something, there is an expression of neediness. When you crave something, and you pursue that craving, you believe your will to choose has been eliminated. When you desire something, you wish for it or want it to happen, but you have to decide to pursue it. Therefore, you have to make the choice to pursue it or follow your desire. When you are driven by your flesh, you believe your freedom of choice has been eliminated, and the choice has been made for you based on the cravings of your sinful nature. Because, when you operate within your flesh, you often believe that you have no choice. When you walk in the Holy Spirit, the freedom of choice is given because you have to choose to follow. You choose what you love. We follow Jesus Christ because we love Him. Love isn't forced, but it is a choice.

Lust can refer to a number of things. You can lust after the opposite sex, or you can strongly crave and lust for alcohol, attention, or approval from others. Whatever struggles we are facing, we must ensure that we do not allow the wrong seeds to be planted within us. What is planted within your mind will take root within your heart. And the fruit of what grows will either nourish you or poison you. If a tree is planted and is exposed to poison, the process of growth will be paralyzed. If you allow the poison of sin to be planted within your mind, it will take root within your heart, and your spiritual growth will be paralyzed. Poison ushers in death; it kills all that it touches. Sin ushers in spiritual death; it kills all that it fills. Our minds must be spaces filled with the fruit and nourishment of God, which is His Word. We must meditate and set our minds on things that are pure and pleasing to the Holy Spirit. We cannot allow our minds to become wastelands of sin. Because what your mind believes, your heart receives; your body follows and will produce the harvest of what is planted within you. So, if lust is planted within you, it will pollute the soil, and what grows will not be fruitful. We must seek and pursue God with the totality of our hearts. It is time to take a stand against the battle within our hearts that has us retreating to raise the white flag of submission. No longer will we run and hide in exile and isolation. No longer will we cower at the battle that is before us. We have recognized the ways in which the enemy wishes to neutralize us internally. Now it is time to develop our strategy and battle plan. Will you stand and fight with me?

Praise the Lord, who is my rock. He trains my hands for war and gives my fingers skill for battle.

—Psalm 144:1 (NLT)

CHAPTER 2

Prepare for Battle

In chapter 1, we discussed the importance of recognizing the battles that we find ourselves in. In this chapter, we will transition to preparing for the battle. Preparation is key when it comes to defending yourself in spiritual warfare. We defend ourselves by first submitting the battle to God. Secondly, we eliminate the temptations around us, or remove ourselves from situations that tempt our flesh to pursue something that would lead to sin. However, there are times when temptations come to us without a welcoming invitation. So let us first define temptation before we proceed. A basic definition of temptation is something that we internally desire or crave. Obviously, there would be no temptation if we did not have a desire for and/or craving for what we are being tempted with. The internal desire is present, and the craving of our carnal appetite drives us to pursue what nourishes our flesh. In order for us to prepare for the battle that is before us, we must take an inventory of what tempts us. When you take an inventory of what your flesh craves or what may have caused you to stumble in the past, you can build a battle plan to prevent the surrender to temptation. Let us prepare a spiritual assessment and checklist. This will be a tool that you can use that will provide you information to help you become self-aware on:

- What tempted you
- What caused you to surrender to the temptation

The assessment can be developed into two versions. The first would be used to prevent you from falling into temptation. The second version would be used to help you understand why you have fallen victim to the temptation.

The first version we will label as pre-sin, and the second version we will label as post-sin.

This is not a way to concede success in the battle; I don't want you to misunderstand the purpose of this. The purpose of this is to prevent you from falling victim to sin. However, if you do fall victim to sin, the second version can help you understand why. If there is one thing I am certain of, it is that the enemy learns from our mistakes—even if we don't. If you are unsure how to answer the questions below, ask the Holy Spirit to reveal the answers to you. Ask God to illuminate your vulnerabilities that you may not be aware of, because preparation for every battle begins in prayer. Go into your war room (place of prayer), and ask God to provide you with the battle plan.

Spiritual Assessment: Pre-Sin

1. What sins have you struggled with in the past?
2. In what areas of your life do you feel vulnerable?
3. Is there any unaddressed trauma from your past?
4. Do you frequently visit places or come across things which cause you to feel vulnerable to temptation?

5. Are you surrounded by people who indulge in things that you struggle with?
6. Are you surrounded by people who encourage healing over medicating your wounds (going to bars, drinking, or using other forms of distraction that do not deal with the issue)?
7. Are you having consistent prayer and devotional time with God? (Because sin often takes place when we have drifted from the presence of God.)
8. Are you a part of an accountability group, or do you have friends whom you trust and can be accountable to?

The pre-sin checklist that you will develop will help you understand the struggles that you have within your life. It will also help you understand some unaddressed issues that may still be lingering from your past. In order to seek true healing, you must search for the root issue. If you cut down a tree at its trunk, in time, it will begin to grow again. You cannot prevent a tree from growing unless you uproot it. If you leave the roots in the soil that provides it with nourishment, it will continue to grow. Therefore, if you allow the roots of your issues to remain in places in which your flesh continues to provide them with nourishment, they will remain rooted within you. These roots will grow into sinful actions. This is why prayer is detrimental to this process, because God can lead you to what is beneath the surface of your struggles. Oftentimes, we can only see what is on the surface, but we are blind to what is beneath it.

Now, let us go into the post-sin spiritual assessment. This is something that I highly encourage you to do if you fall victim to temptation.

Spiritual Assessment: Post-Sin

1. Have you repented to God and accepted accountability for your mistake(s)?
2. Did you attempt to pray and call to God for help?
3. Where were you when you committed this sin, and what were you doing?
4. How were you feeling when you committed this sin?
5. Were you alone or isolated when you committed this sin?

6. Was this sin provoked by the people you surrounded yourself with?
7. Did you try leaving the area to avoid the temptation? In other cases, did you leave the immediate area to attempt to do a reset (which means go to another place to compose yourself)?
8. Did you try to contact your accountability partner or group?
9. Knowing what you know now, what could you have done differently?
10. First, submit the results of this assessment to God in prayer. Then discuss the answers of this assessment with your accountability partner.

We are designing this to bring more spiritual self-awareness to the battles of temptation that we face in our walk of faith. I encourage you to use this assessment, or develop one that is unique to you and your situation. By completing a checklist such as this, you will begin to see receive clarity into the how and why of falling victim to temptation. It gives you the ability to learn and understand what you must do to prevent yourself from stumbling or falling into sin. For example, it gives you a blueprint to recognize your triggers, so you will know when it is time to remove yourself from those situations. If you are not aware of your triggers, you will not realize you are in a battle until it is too late. The battle consumes you when you are not prepared for it. Defeat is certain if you do not have a battle plan. Think of it this way: when you trip and stumble over something, the first instinctive reaction is to analyze what you tripped over. Without hesitation, you shift your line of sight to search for what caused you to lose balance.

This assessment is a way to escape shame and guilt, and to shift your focus to what may have caused you to lose balance in your purity or whatever it is that you are struggling with. As followers of Jesus, our hearts break when we feel as if we have taken His sacrifice in vain. Our hearts break at the thought of committing sin within the sight of God. Our hearts break at the thought of ignoring the Holy Spirit and proceeding to wander down this path that has led us to falter in our walk of faith. Lying in the debris of our sin, in the aftermath of our rebellion, is where we find ourselves paralyzed in sorrow. This posture is what we have to climb out of because we cannot remain in our brokenness. Therefore, I recommend placing both assessments somewhere that is readily assessable so that in these moments you can see them and:

1. Be reminded of the situations to avoid placing yourself in them.
2. Get to the root cause of what has transpired so that you may not stumble in this way again.

In regard to the checklist, this can be something that is totally unique to you but, I will give you an example of what my checklist is.

Spiritual Checklist

- Put God first (begin my day with prayer and time in God's Word).
- Focus my thoughts on what is pure and holy.
- Do not place myself in situations that will cause me to react in sinful ways.

- Remember who I am in Christ, and that my identity is in Jesus.
- Do not allow my physical space to determine who I am spiritually (for example, allowing where I am to change who I am based on my job or the places I go throughout the day).
- Be quick to listen, slow to speak, and slow to anger (James 1:19 ([NLT]).
- Do not allow others to control my emotions or reactions.
- Be intentional with my time. Time is currency that is nonrefundable. Once it is spent, it cannot be returned.
- Go for a midday walk and pray.
- Remind myself that I am not defined by my past sins and mistakes.
- End my day with God, and surrender all that happened throughout the day to Him.

Developing a checklist such as this will provide you with constant reminders to help you remain anchored in your faith in God. The items on your checklist also serve as helpful parameters to ensure you do not place yourself in a battle. They build a foundation of keeping God first in your life. We live in constant movement, in a world that captures our focus. Therefore, it is important to have a checklist that can remind you throughout the day to center yourself spiritually. We venture into our days with uncertainty of what may transpire throughout the day. We place our faith in God, and we trust in Him to order our steps on the paths that we will traverse. However, placing a checklist such as this at your desk, in your car, or wherever you spend the majority of your time throughout the day will ensure you do not allow the events of the day to dictate who you are throughout the day.

Time is currency that is nonrefundable. Once it is spent, it cannot be returned.

Pause, and take a few moments here to pray and seek God for the information to develop your own assessments and checklist.

Now that you have developed your own assessments and checklist, you have taken an important step in preparing for the battle. You have surveyed the horizon and scouted the battlefield for all potential threats to your walk of faith. As you look out into the fog of the unknown with uncertainty of what lies beyond it, you can stand in absolute faith and confidence without fear. Why? Because the God of all creation stands with you, and you have taken necessary steps to ensure that you will remain prepared for whatever battle the enemy may send your way in the days to come. Make no mistake; preparing for battle is a daily strategy session with God. This is where you have to go to your war room—or battle-ready room, as I like to call it. You have to remain in a posture of a constant pursuit of God. I want to be very clear: none of what you read above will be able to help you if you do not put God first and allow Him to direct your battle plan. What I have given you is a practical example, but your personal preparations for battle need to come from the Lord, who fights our battles for us.

No assessment or checklist can protect you without God. For we look to the Heavens for help. "I look up to the mountains—does my help come from there? My help comes from the Lord, who made heaven and earth! He will not let you stumble; the one who watches over you will not slumber" (Psalm 121:1–3 [NLT]). The Lord is our help, and He is who watches over us constantly. We never escape His sight; He sees all and knows all. God knows the battles, struggles, and troubles that we face. Therefore, seek Him for the preparation of your battle, and allow His Holy Spirit to guide you in the creation of barriers and parameters that you will place within your life to avoid straying onto a wrong path. God will help us and give us strength, but we have to make the conscious choice to receive it. God has given us the freedom of choice and the freedom to choose Him. He doesn't make the decision for us; this is why we have to remain vigilant and not become prideful. This is why we have to partner with Him to ensure we are doing everything we can to live lives that are pleasing to Him. We were each created for a purpose in this world, and it is time we take back the lives God created us to live. You are not defined by the sins of yesterday.

So go into this day focused on God and the purpose He created you for.

Put on all of God's armor so that you will be able to stand firm against all strategies of the devil.

—Ephesians 6:11–12 (NLT)

CHAPTER 3

Armed for Battle

In chapter 1, we learned how to recognize the different battles that we face in life. In chapter 2, we learned how to prepare for the battles that are before us. Now we will learn how to arm ourselves for battle. If you are like me, the title of this chapter immediately shifted your attention to the armor of God. And rightfully so, as this is how we as followers of Christ arm ourselves for battle. However, before we go into the armor of God, I want to bring an often-overlooked verse to your attention. In Ephesians chapter 6, there is a verse that gives us a clear

> We need the strength of the Lord to remain anchored in place when the hurricane winds of temptation come to sink us.

direction prior to outfitting ourselves with God's armor. The verse that I am speaking of is verse 10, and it reads: "A final word: Be strong in the Lord and in His mighty power" (Ephesians 6:10 [NLT]). The apostle Paul was directing the church in Ephesus to not move in their own strength. Prior to the outfitting of the armor, Paul made it very clear that you must first be strong in the Lord and His mighty power.

The armor of God cannot be utilized effectively if we move in our own strength. Therefore, we must be strong in the Lord and His mighty power. God is the epicenter and the central focus for every believer. He is the foundation and must remain so. In verse 10, the word power in the Greek translation is *dunamis*. *Dunamis* basically translates to power, or ability—and we have to trust in the power and ability of God. We are limited in what we can do without God in our defense against the enemy in spiritual warfare. We need the strength of the Lord to remain anchored in place when the hurricane winds of temptation come to sink us. Otherwise, we will be overtaken by the waves of despair and discouragement that will crash into us from every direction with the sole purpose of taking us deep into the abyss to drown us in our own hubris. There are times in our spiritual warfare when we may feel as if we can barely keep our face above the surface. We are gasping for air, with every breath becoming a struggle to absorb the essential air we need to survive. What is unseen beneath the surface is the weight of our past mistakes, shame, and guilt wrapped around us. We begin to grow weaker and weaker by the moment, and the strength we once had to remain above the surface has been exhausted. The belt that our past sins and mistakes are attached to is the belt of lies from the enemy.

This belt of lies is the weight that is threatening to take us deeper and deeper into the darkness because this belt tells a story of lies that is being narrated by the father of lies. Attached to this belt are lies such as:

- You are not worth saving.
- You will never be free of this.
- Why are you trying to evade the life you know you want to live?
- God doesn't love you. If He did, why would He allow this to happen to you?
- You have no calling or purpose in life.

The lies of the enemy are endless. He is the source of lies with an infinite supply of deceit, disruptions, and distractions. On your path to purpose, he will offer you many side roads of distraction. These offtrack paths will normally be found in things that our flesh craves, or he will use those who are close to us to disrupt and distract us. In order to stay the course, we must combat the lies of the enemy with the truth of God. His truth is His Word, and it will tear down every stronghold and lie of the enemy. So now we will venture into the different components of the armor of God and how they can protect us against the fiery arrows of the enemy, which can be found in Ephesians chapter 6, verses 10–17.

The components of the *full* armor of God are:

- The belt of truth
- The breastplate of righteousness
- The shoes of peace
- The shield of faith
- The helmet of salvation
- The sword of the Spirit
- *Bonus secret weapon:* pray in the Spirit at all times (Ephesians 6:18 [NLT])

I want to discuss specifically the belt of truth and how it holds all of the armor of God together.

The Belt of Truth

> Stand your ground, putting on the belt of truth and the body armor of God's righteousness.
>
> —**Ephesians 6:14 (NLT)**

In the order of instructions as it pertains to the outfitting of the armor of God, I find it very interesting that the belt of truth would be the first piece that is donned as armor. The belt is what would be used to hold the weapon. Therefore, it would most commonly be donned as one of the final pieces. Wouldn't it make more sense to put on the breastplate of righteousness first? It seems like the more logical choice, right? However, I began to look at the particular order of outfitting from a different perspective. I had to move beyond the label of the piece of clothing (the belt) to see what type of belt is mentioned. It is called the belt of truth, and truth is what holds the armor together. It strengthens every component of your armor by strengthening your faith in that particular piece. So what is truth in this context? The truth is God's Word because He is the truth, and this is what we are being told to equip ourselves with first. Because if you are not equipped with the Word and truth of God in your heart, you will not have faith in the remaining components of the armor. If you do not don the Word of God, you will not believe that you are righteous when your past sins and mistakes tell a different story. You will believe that your past is still a nonfiction story in your present. That continues to tell the narrative that you are not—and never will be—righteous.

However, God's Word, His truth, says otherwise.

In chapter 5 in the book of Romans, it begins with the statement that we are made right in God's sight by faith. Specifically, it says, "Therefore, since we have been made right in God's sight by faith, we have peace with God because of what Jesus Christ our Lord has done for us" (Romans 5:1 [NLT]). The word "right" in this context means righteous. We are all made righteous in God's sight by placing our faith in Jesus Christ. By having faith, and knowing this, we can put on the breastplate of righteousness with absolute confidence because we believe that we are righteous through Jesus Christ's sacrifice for us. If we do not fill ourselves with the truth of God as it pertains to peace, we will believe that it is an unattainable fantasy during the difficult seasons in our lives. The truth is that we have a peace that surpasses all peace and understanding, and that peace comes from Jesus Christ. We have this peace when we live and rest in Jesus. You will see this in the book of Philippians, which says, "Don't worry about anything; instead, pray about everything. Tell God what you need, and thank him for all he has done. Then you will experience God's peace, which exceeds anything we can understand. His peace will guard your hearts and minds as you live in Christ Jesus" (Philippians 4:6–7 [NLT]).

What the world offers us is a false peace wrapped within the vices that provide some form of medication for our vulnerabilities and insecurities. We run and seek refuge in the things that bring what we believe to be some form of soothing escape from what we are dealing with in our lives, whether it be rejection, addiction, or an unfruitful season in which we are barely keeping our face above the surface. Verse 6 of chapter 4 in the book of Philippians tells us to not worry about anything but to instead pray about everything. Submit our needs to God, and thank Him for all that He has done. This is how we can have peace. When you begin to pray and submit all that is troubling you to God, you are not internalizing whatever is troubling you. You are not holding it in but are releasing it to God, who already knows what is troubling you and/or what you are struggling with. God just wants you to come and talk to Him about it. When you begin to thank Him for all that He has done, it brings forth remembrance of all the things that He has brought you through. Then you can have peace because you know that if He did it before, He can and will certainly do it again in accordance with His will for your life.

Believing God's truth (His Word) is also having faith in it and all it pertains to. Therefore, by placing my faith in His Word and that it is in fact truth, it can be used as a shield to defend me against the lies of the enemy. Hence, it is the shield of faith that protects us from the fiery arrows of the enemy. Having faith in His Word provides a shield of protection for every believer. I have come to find, through my own experiences in my walk of faith, that the enemy loves to focus on our identities and what our flesh craves the most. His tactics are not something that is bewildering beyond our understanding but are calculated. The enemy will offer you something that your flesh craves, and he will use that very thing against you to shame you. I will give you an example:

> **The enemy:** I know that you've had a pretty rough day. You should watch pornography to help you relax.
>
> **Chris:** That is not something that is pleasing to God, nor is that who I am anymore.

The enemy: You need this release to help you decompress because you don't want to project your frustrations out against your wife, right?

Chris: (Sits in silence.)

The enemy: Your exact words that you constantly repeat to others are, "I don't want to take work home. My time at home is the time that I am giving to my family." This will help you not take work home and be true to what you are speaking.

Chris: (Surrenders to the flesh and acts out.)

The enemy: How can you be called to ministry when you can't obey the Word of God that you are preaching? You are a hypocrite, and you are not called and/or anointed by God.

If I allow myself to believe the lies of the enemy, even in the aftermath of my sin, I will believe that I am not worthy of God's grace and mercy. I will believe that I am beyond redemption, and that I will never conquer my struggles and vulnerabilities. However, God's Word is perfectly clear that "Each time he said, 'My grace is all you need. My power works best in weakness.' So now I am glad to boast about my weaknesses, so that the power of Christ can work through me. That's why I take pleasure in my weaknesses, and in the insults, hardships, persecutions, and troubles that I suffer for Christ. For when I am weak, then I am strong" (2 Corinthians 12:9–10 [NLT]).

The above Scripture tells me that I cannot defeat my addiction on my own strength. It is the power that Jesus gives me through His Holy Spirit that empowers me to conquer the sin in my life. God's grace is sufficient for all of my mistakes, vulnerabilities, and weaknesses. We live empowered lives by the power of the Holy Spirit that lives within us. We are able to cut through every lie of the enemy and tear down every stronghold within our lives. With that being said, let us talk about the sword of the Spirit. A sword is an offensive weapon. Yes, it can also block attacks, but its primary use is for offense. A shield is a defensive weapon to block attacks, but a sword is a weapon used to commit attacks. When the sword is sharp, it can pierce and cut through anything. It becomes a very dangerous weapon in the hand of the warrior or soldier who wields it. The Bible is our weapon as believers in spiritual warfare. It is our offensive weapon against the traps, attacks, and ambushes the enemy has set for us. You can begin your offensive in spiritual warfare when you equip yourself with the sword of the Spirit, which is God's living and breathing Word.

In regard to the armor of God, Ephesians chapter 6, verse 18, is a verse that is normally left out of this concept. I would argue that is the protective seal of the armor of God. Verse 18 says, "Pray in the Spirit at all times and on every occasion. Stay alert and be persistent in your prayers for all believers everywhere" (Ephesians 6:18 [NLT]). Praying in the Spirit is the secret weapon for all believers and followers of Christ. I am not talking about speaking in tongues or unknown languages specifically, but allowing the Holy Spirit to control the direction of your prayers and what you are praying for. This is something that is very essential for our prayer life. We do not always know what to pray for, but the Holy Spirit—who is in perfect harmony with God does know—what we should pray for. You can read this in Romans chapter 8, which specifies that the Holy Spirit helps us in our inability to find the correct words to pray or what to pray for. "And the Holy Spirit helps us in our weakness. For example, we don't know what God wants us to pray for. But the Holy Spirit prays for us with groanings that cannot be expressed in words. And the Father who knows all hearts knows what the Spirit is saying, for the Spirit pleads for us believers in harmony with God's own will" (Romans 8:26–27 [NLT]). Therefore, if we are to be alert and persistent in our prayers, we must allow the Holy Spirit to lead our prayers.

I mentioned the gift of tongues, or as some would call it, our prayer language. This is a very powerful gift that I believe every believer should pursue and seek God for. This is a gift the modern church doesn't speak about anymore, as it makes modern Christian uncomfortable. You have to truly understand what takes place in this moment to understand its power. When you begin to speak in your prayer language, this is a heavenly language that is only understood by God. This is a conversation that is taking place between the Holy Spirit and God on your behalf.

I don't know about you, but I do not want to suppress something as beautiful and powerful as this. The Holy Spirit within me is talking to God for me. This is how we can be prepared for things we do not know are coming. This is how we can remain alert for ourselves and for those who are connected to us. We may not know everything that is going on in the lives of everyone who is connected to us, but God does. So, if you have not prayed in tongues (or you have, but you have suppressed it because you feared others may say), I encourage you to begin this practice by allowing the Holy Spirit to guide your prayers and pray on your behalf.

We use God's mighty weapons, not worldly weapons, to knock down the strongholds of human reasoning and to destroy false arguments.

—2 Corinthians 10:4 (NLT)

CHAPTER 4

Spiritual Warriors

When you hear the term warrior, what image fills your mind? What does this warrior look like? What attributes does this warrior display? Is this warrior a person of absolute bravery, who will not retreat in the face of danger? Does this warrior have a very intimidating stature that would bring fear to the hearts of his enemies? Does this warrior yield a mighty weapon that will strike down all who oppose him? We each have images of what we believe a warrior should look like and the power that a warrior should have. This is due to the way people perceive what a warrior should be, based on the standards created by movies and/or television shows. Hollywood has given us a worldly blueprint for what it means to be brave, courageous, and a warrior who decimates his enemies. However, as followers of Christ, we know that we cannot defeat the enemy on our own strength. We know we have no power apart from God to break down demonic strongholds or enter into battle with spiritual warfare. A spiritual warrior is not someone who can conquer enemies, destroy strongholds, or win the battle of spiritual warfare on their own strength. In this chapter, I want to change your perception of what you believe a warrior is. In faith, I hope to accomplish this by showing you how God has used some of the least likely people to do the most miraculous things.

However, before we go into these mighty people from biblical history, let us first venture into the epigraph for this chapter. This epigraph is from the text of 2 Corinthians, and it reads: "We use God's mighty weapons, not worldly weapons, to knock down the strongholds of human reasoning and to destroy false arguments" (2 Corinthians 10:4 [NLT]). Paul is writing to the church of Corinth, and in this particular text, we first see that we use God's mighty weapons, not worldly weapons. This is powerful because it is the only way to address human reasoning and to destroy false arguments. So what are these weapons? We can find those weapons in Ephesians chapter 6; specifically, verses 17 and 18. It reads: "Put on salvation as your helmet, and take the sword of the Spirit, which is the word of God. Pray in the Spirit at all times, and on every occasion. Stay alert and persistent in your prayers for all believers everywhere" (Ephesians 6:17–18 [NLT]). The weapons of God that we have access to are His Word and prayer. We cannot use worldly weapons against spiritual warfare. Spiritual warfare is a battle that is fought with spiritual weapons. Therefore, we approach human reasoning and false arguments with the weapons that we have access to through God. So let us discuss how the mighty weapons of God can combat human reasoning and false arguments.

Human Reasoning

Human reasoning is the way we approach things logically, and it affects the way we perceive or receive things. We cannot understand the things of God with our own reasoning because our reasoning will dismiss anything spiritually that we do not understand and/or grasp the concept of. So what are the pitfalls or the fallout of that? When we make a mistake and sin against God, if we see our mistake through the lens of our reasoning, we will believe we are not worthy of forgiveness because our mistake becomes amplified if we are only seeing it through the lens of our own perspective. Also, we will venture to believe the struggles that we have in our lives are inescapable. The longer we have been engulfed within these struggles, the more illogical our thinking becomes. We will find ourselves in a war of words and lies against ourselves. We will use the lies of the enemy as weapons against the freedom that Christ has given us. In this posture and/or way of thinking, you will find yourself saying things like, "I have struggled with this for too long. There is no way that I can be free of this. This sin or vice has too much power over me." By doing this, you are attributing the length of time that you have struggled with how difficult you believe it will be to gain freedom from it. Because of the length of time you have struggled, you see this as an inescapable prison, a death sentence to your hopes of freedom.

This is when using the mighty weapons of God become very important and/or critical to aligning our way of thinking to what God says about us. First, I want to say there is no sin that has more power than Jesus Christ. For the Scriptures say, "And since we died with Christ, we know we will also live with him. We are sure of this because Christ was raised from the dead, and he will never die again. Death no longer has any power over him. When he died, he died once to break the power of sin. But now that he lives, he lives for the glory of God. So you also should consider yourselves to be dead to the power of sin and alive to God through Christ Jesus" (Romans 6:8–11 [NLT]). Therefore, since we believe that God's Word is truth, we know that Jesus Christ broke the power of sin. The Scriptures continue to say that "you also should consider yourselves to be dead to the power of sin and alive to God through Christ Jesus." The Holy Spirit raised us from spiritual death when Jesus Christ entered our hearts. There is no sin that has more power than Jesus Christ who lives in you. A struggle is not a sign of defeat but a sign of transformation. A struggle means there is resistance in areas of your life where there was none before. Find joy in the fact that you have a struggle, because this means that you are not defeated but are still fighting. We are told in Romans chapter 12 to be transformed by the renewal of our minds. The way that we are able to defeat our own flawed reasoning is by allowing the Holy Scriptures to transform our minds. Once we begin to renew our minds, and allow the lies we believe to be transformed into truth, we can begin to live transformed lives. We will begin to break through the barriers of human reasoning to see that all things are possible with God (Matthew 19:26 [NLT]).

The other weapon that we have is prayer; specifically, praying in the Spirit, as it is written in Ephesians chapter 6. I spoke about this in a previous chapter, but it is important to reiterate this in regard to how we combat human reasoning. So how do we combat the things that we do not understand or cannot perceive with our limited human perception and/or intellect? By submitting them to the God who knows all things—the omniscient, all-knowing God—through prayer. For God is eternal and limitless in all things. There is no physical or spiritual way for us to know all things, but God is the one who does know all things. So, if we find ourselves in a wilderness of reasoning that we cannot seem to escape, we need to call on the Lord to help us. We call on God so that He can help us navigate the deserted areas of our own understanding, because it is often barren of the answers we need. This is why prayer is so essential to our relationship with God. It is a coming together, to speak with the God of the universe about the things that are within our minds and hearts, the things that rage within us like hurricane winds that destroy all

> We call on God so that He can help us navigate the deserted areas of our own understanding, because it is often barren of the answers we need.

peace within their path. If there is one thing that I am certain of, it is that Jesus Christ has the power to calm any storm. He controls the winds and the waves with the sound of His voice. Therefore, He can heal you with whatever is raging inside you, and He can bring peace to areas of your life that have been absent of it.

False Arguments

False arguments in this context can be seen as false philosophies, or doctrines that do not align with biblical Scripture. In a world of many different religions, it is important to absorb the Word of God so that we can be disciples for Christ, led by His Holy Spirit to lead people to Him. However, we also need to absorb the Word of God for our own spiritual protection. We do not want to find ourselves swept up by a whirlwind of false teaching that leads us astray. It is not only those who are lost who need the clarity of Scriptures to guide their lives; we who are in Christ need it, as well. The society we live in today is a world of constant debate and rebuke. When you find yourself going into the corridors of any social platform, you are likely to see a debate and/or reaction videos to current events. These events are those that happen within the church and outside of the church, led by those who devote their time to giving their opinions based on what they believe to be fact. This is why it is critical and essential to immerse ourselves into the Word of God. If we do not know and understand the Holy Scriptures for ourselves, we will find ourselves following the doctrines of personality and charisma. I will provide some clarity to this. People are drawn to the personalities of people they can relate to. For example, I grew up fatherless, and I have dealt with rejection and sexual sin (in the form of a pornography addiction). If I was to host a biblical podcast, those who have walked the path that I have walked may be drawn to me because I am relatable to their story, and because I have similar issues as the ones they have dealt with or are currently dealing with.

Their desire to be free could blind them from seeing whether the information I am actually giving them is fruitful. I could be providing false philosophies or false doctrines by speaking from the Scriptures out of context, and they would take what I say as truth. This is what happens when wolves who disguise themselves as shepherds wish to monetize the vulnerabilities of others. If I cannot decipher and interpret the words that I am receiving as truths or lies, I will be following a wolf who is leading me farther away from God. Do not be drawn to trends and charisma. You need to ensure that you are able to exercise discernment, to ensure you are not walking a path that will lead you deeper into your vulnerabilities. False arguments can also be related to what is known as apologetics. The word apologetics comes from the Greek word *apologia*, which means defense. Apologetics is basically defending your faith. This is going to help you, I promise, so follow me on this topic for a moment. In order to defend your faith in Jesus Christ, you will not only have to gain knowledge on who Jesus Christ is, but you will have to be able to defend your findings and beliefs. Therefore, you will have to know the Word of God to defend the faith against not only other religions but those who are atheist as well. You will have to help those who do not believe in God to receive in their hearts that there is, in fact, a God. People who have this calling on their lives fill themselves with the Word of God (as we all should). Which means, the more of the truth of God you have in you, the less room you leave in your heart for the lies of the enemy. Loading our hearts with spiritual ammo will help us defend ourselves in the battles that we find ourselves in.

Having faith in the truth of God gives us the courage and boldness that we need to face the giants that are blocking our path to purpose and victory. Now I want to venture into history to talk about some of the least likely people whom God used to do very miraculous things. People whom God used to conquer the giant(s) who inflicted fear and persecution onto His people include:

1. Moses
2. David
3. Gideon

Moses

Moses was born as a Hebrew slave. When Moses was a baby, the pharaoh of Egypt was slaughtering all male babies as they were born. He gave the order to the midwives of

Egypt to kill the baby if it was a boy, and to allow it to live if it was a girl. To save his life, Moses's mother placed him into a basket and onto the Nile River. As he floated upriver, he was pulled out of the river by the daughter of the pharaoh. This is the origin of his name, as the name Moses means to "pull out, or draw out," Moses was raised in the palace of the pharaoh, until one day, he saw an Egyptian guard beating a Hebrew slave. Moses killed the guard, and he fled Egypt because he was fearful that the pharaoh would kill him. Moses spent the next forty years in the wilderness, a self-imposed exile from the life he used to know. He took refuge in a foreign land because the place he knew was no longer home. In this wilderness, Moses had an encounter with God that would change his life. One day, as he pursued a sheep who went astray from his flock, he found himself on Mount Sinai. He went up the mountain to pursue and find his stray sheep, but he found something else. He encountered a burning bush, and the voice of God called out to Moses and gave him an assignment to go back to Egypt so that God could use him to free his people (Exodus 3:1–22 [NLT]).

Moses provided God with many excuses as to why he should not be used for such a task as this. He saw himself as unworthy, and he began to point out things that he believed would disqualify him from this calling. Regardless of what Moses tried to use to justify his reasoning to not submit to the calling, God had an answer. For every inadequacy Moses pointed out, God reminded him that it was He who would accomplish this task through Moses. Moses, who left Egypt as a murderer, would return to become a liberator. During this assignment, God did many miraculous things that would lead to the exodus (mass departure) of the Israelites from Egypt. God used Moses regardless of his inadequacies, past sins, or qualifications. God can use you to go forth in any assignment He has for you, regardless of how you see yourself or what you have done. Your past does not measure the volume of your effectiveness in God's Kingdom. The battles that you are in will not overcome you. The same God who was with Moses in Egypt, and in the wilderness in the aftermath of the exodus from Egypt, is with you. You know who Moses is because he agreed to go back to a place that once tried to kill him as a baby, a place that became home to him and then wanted to kill him again. You know who Daniel is because he did not tell God to remove the lions, but he remained among the lions and allowed God to do what he couldn't do. Therefore, God will show up in your situation and do what seems impossible to you.

David

A shepherd in the pastures of Bethlehem would become the king of Israel. I don't want to remind you of the anointing to be king, or how he was rejected and was not invited to the coronation in his father's house. What I want to point out to you is a very familiar story: the battle between David and Goliath. Goliath was a Philistine who taunted the army of Israel and spoke evil against God for forty days and nights. David was back home with his father, Jesse, stewarding over the flock of sheep that had been entrusted to him. Jesse instructed David to go to the battlefield to take food to the captains of the army, and to speak with his brothers. Once this was completed, he was told to return to his father with a report of what was happening. However, once David arrived at the battlefield, he heard the taunts of Goliath, and he volunteered to go into battle. Yes, the shepherd from the pastures of Bethlehem had volunteered to fight the strongest warrior in the Philistine army. Saul received news of this, and after a back-and-forth discussion, he agreed to allow David to fight Goliath. This is important: Saul wanted to equip David with what he thought would give David a better chance of success. He wished to outfit David with his armor, but David quickly realized that he could not fight in Saul's armor (1 Samuel 17:32–37 [NLT]).

David went into battle as he was, not as who someone else thought he should be. He went into the valley with the weapons of a shepherd, not a soldier. He used the very same things to defeat Goliath as he used to defend his flock from wild animals who wished to attack them. The same sling, equipped with a rock, subdued a mighty warrior. At that moment, David would use the very weapon that Goliath would use against him to kill him. This is what I want you to understand. You don't have to equip yourself with all of the things that you think have made other people successful in conquering their giants. The only thing God needs is your submission to Him, to come to Him as He created you, and not as a replica of someone else. If you come to Him as who you are, and you are vulnerable in His presence, He can and will slay the giants that are blocking your pathway to purpose, deliverance, or healing. The weapons the enemy formed to use against you will not prosper, just as the sword of Goliath did not prosper against David. Sometimes, all it takes is a shepherd to slay a giant.

Gideon

Gideon's story is both powerful and very interesting. Gideon was someone from biblical history who showed us that it is OK to ask for confirmation from God. I believe that Gideon encountered what is known as a Christophany, which means it was not a messenger angel who appeared in Judges chapter 6 and said, "Mighty hero, the Lord is with you" (Judges 6:12 [NLT]). I believe it was Jesus Himself who appeared to Gideon. Gideon was called by God to deliver His people from the oppression and persecution of the Midianites. What is so amazing about this story is that Gideon originally had an army of twenty thousand soldiers, which was decreased to three hundred soldiers. God gave Gideon specific instructions on what to do as he approached the camp of the Midianites. Once they took their assigned positions, they blew their ram horns, broke their clay jars, and shouted, "A sword for the Lord, and for Gideon" (Judges 7:19–20 [NLT]). Once the sound of their ram horns echoed throughout the camp, the Midianites began to fight each other. This is what I want you to see: God will place you in position for the battle, to watch Him fight the battle for you. Gideon followed the instructions and directions that he had been given by God, and He caused the army to fight themselves. This is the Lord fighting our battles for us. I want to encourage you that it does not matter how difficult the seasons of your life have been; God can show up and give you victory. The Bible provides us with example after example of how God protects us, fights for us, and gives us victory. Faith in God is our ammunition, and it is the only weapon that we will ever need.

For God has not given us a spirit of fear and timidity, but of power, love, and self-discipline.

—2 Timothy 1:7 (NLT)

CHAPTER 5

Never Retreat

I think we can all agree that victory is not won from a position of retreat. In order for victory to be attained, we must face the battle that is before us. We must have the courage to go behind enemy lines in order to subdue the adversary that withholds the promise of victory from us. So the technical definition of retreat is to withdraw from enemy forces as a result of their superior power or after a defeat. Therefore, to retreat is to accept two things:

1. The enemy is superior.
2. You accept, or you have been defeated.

Do you have the faith in God to remain in battle, even if the enemy has raided your sight of all hopes of victory? The mantra "never retreat" reminds me of this one secular show I used to watch years ago. The show that I am referring to is *Game of Thrones*. In this particular show, there was a scene in which a battle raged on between two sides. One side was completely decimated, with only one faithful soldier (Jon Snow) remaining. The battlefield was immersed in a thick fog, and the sun was drowned out by smoke and haze. The enemy's army began to ride fiercely to Jon's position. Instead of retreating, he grabbed his sword with both hands and prepared to fight until his last breath. I can imagine his heart was pounding, and his eyes saw what was certain defeat barreling toward him. With his feet planted into the earth beneath him, his eyes focused on certain death closing in on him. As he prepared to fight one last time, at the last possible moment, help arrived to secure his victory. I know that I paraphrased this scene in a small sum of words. However, what I want you to see in this is that, even when he was the only soldier left, he did not retreat. He was willing to fight until his death.

There are people in the Bible that you and I both know because God did not take them out of the situations they were in. He saw them through those situations. Our remembrances of them are based on the hardships they overcame. We would not know their names if they had not faced what was before them. Therefore, let us first discuss Hananiah, Mishael, and Azariah. You may know them by the names they were given as slaves of Babylon, Shadrach, Meshach, and Abednego. In the book of Daniel, chapter 3, King Nebuchadnezzar had a gold statue of himself constructed. It was the king's order for this statue to be worshipped when the sound of music filled the atmosphere. Once the music played, all who were under the sound of it would bow to the statue and worship the king. This was a direct violation of the First Commandment which states: "You shall have no other gods before Me" (Exodus 20:3 [New King James Version]). To bow to this statue was to break the First Commandment. This was idolatry, a sin that Hananiah, Mishael, and Azariah were determined not to commit. So, when the music played, they refused to bow and worship the king. This filled Nebuchadnezzar with rage, and he offered them another chance to bow down and worship him. Their response was so powerful. They replied to Nebuchadnezzar and said, "O Nebuchadnezzar, we do not need to defend ourselves before you. If we are thrown into the blazing furnace, the God whom we serve is able to save us. He will rescue us from your power, Your Majesty. But even if he doesn't, we want to make it clear to you, Your Majesty, that we will never serve your gods or worship the gold statue you have set up" (Daniel 3:16–18 [NLT]).

Faced with certain death, they did not waver in their faith. They had the opportunity to retreat from the battle of faith they were currently in. Instead, they stood their ground, even if it meant they would die on that day. They did not retreat, nor did they surrender. Imagine hearing the words that give the order for your execution. The words that sing a symphony of death, echoing from the vocal cords of the king, to some of his strongest soldiers. The order was given to set ablaze a fire that was seven times hotter than any fire they had lit before. Imagine standing there and hearing all of those words penetrate your hearing. As these sounds enter your hearing, there is a choice to make. To continue to have faith in God, and not surrender, or to submit to the enemy. As the fire was set ablaze, and they were being led to the fire, I can imagine the heat could have been felt from afar. As they drew closer and closer to the fire, what awaited them became clearer. Their eyes were capturing the sight of what would be a torturous death, gruesome in nature. However, they still did not surrender. Their faith in God gave them the strength they needed to face the fire that was lit to exhaust their lives from existence. I can imagine the words that were growing within their hearts, a harvest of prayers to God to come down and save them, or to be with them until their last breath. What was happening in that moment did not escape the sight of God.

They were thrown into the fire, and Jesus Christ, preincarnate, showed up Himself to save them (Christophany) (Daniel 3:25 [NLT]). This is an example that, no matter what fires we may find ourselves in, if we hold tightly to our faith, God will show up. We serve and worship God because of who He is, and not because of the season of life we are in. Our faith is not determined by the victory that we have been given, but it is determined by knowing that God is with us through it all. They said the God whom they serve would be able to save them, and He would rescue them from the king's power. God is able to do all things, and He can save us from all things if it is in His will to do so. Do you have the faith that Hananiah, Mishael, and Azariah had? Yes, they were rescued, but before they were thrown into the fire, they said, "Even if He doesn't." These four words displayed how strong their faith was in God. They wanted the king to know that, even if He didn't save them, they would never worship the king. If we connect our faith to victory, in the face of losses, we will believe we are fighting on our own. Let me make one thing perfectly clear: a

> **Our faith is not determined by the victory that we have been given, but it is determined by knowing that God is with us through it all.**

loss is not defeat. Battles can be lost, and a war can still be won. There may be seasons of your life when you feel as if you have been losing over and over, as if victory is a mirage or a hallucination that is brought on by the weariness of your heart. Jesus said, "Come to me all who are weary, and carry heavy burdens, and I will give you rest" (Matthew 11:28 [NLT]).

We find rest and peace in Jesus, our Lord and Savior, who has already given us victory. He has already subdued the enemy and won the battle for us. No matter if you think you are losing, or you feel as if you have had multiple losing seasons, let me remind you that you follow a God who has never lost. If you abide in Christ, you are winning, and your days of losing are over. Do you have faith in the fire, or does the fire consume your faith and belief that the God of possibility can do the impossible for you? No matter if you are one soldier on a battlefield against a vast army, or if you are thrown into the fire, God can save you. Seasons may change, but our God remains the same.

As time passed by, and one year faded into another, Babylon now had a new king. King Darius of Persia now ruled over the city that oppressed the Israelites and held them captive. Among the captives was a prophet of God named Daniel. He was a friend of the three who had been rescued from the fire. Serving as a prophet of God would require Daniel to be in prayer and constant communion with God. However, this was threatened by a decree that was signed by the king, which can be found in Daniel chapter 6. It is important first to point out the reason this decree was created and signed. Daniel, who was favored by God, caused the other officials to be filled with jealousy.

They could not find fault to accuse him, so they wanted to use his religion and his relationship with God against him. They carefully and intentionally formed the perfect trap to be used against one who was fully submitted to God. A person who has a heart for God cannot go a single day without speaking to Him. So they sought to attack the thing they know he loved more than any other object in this world: his relationship with God. Therefore, the officials convinced the king to temporarily ban prayer for thirty days. Violating this decree was punishable by what could be seen as certain death as the violator would be thrown into the den of lions. Daniel could not, nor did he desire to, go a single day without talking with God. Instead of folding to the tension he found himself in, he did not compromise his relationship with God. Surrendering to this decree was accepting defeat. Daniel did not retreat from this tension, nor did he submit to defeat by silencing his prayers for thirty days. All the while, he knew it meant that if he was discovered, he would be thrown into the den of lions. Is the tension that you may currently be in smothering you with a false belief that defeat is better, especially if it is temporary? Daniel understood this ban was for only thirty days, but he also understood that speaking with God was better than losing his life. He did not want to lose his connection to the one who gave him life. If we allow our vision to see and our minds to believe that defeat is temporary, we will fold to the tension just to relieve the struggles that we are going through.

So Daniel refused to abide by the decree and submit to the prayer ban. Once the king was notified of this, his officials urged him to cast Daniel into the lion's den. After all, he could not go against the decree he had signed into law, no matter how much he wanted to. Imagine being Daniel, and as you are arrested and led to the lion's den, you can hear the roars of the lions. As the door opens, you are thrown into this den of death, an object to satisfy the hunger of the famished lions that dwell within. The door closes, and darkness consumes all light in the room. You are unaware of the moment when you will be attacked, and you're unaware of which lion will strike first. I can imagine that, in this moment, Daniel was praying to God, just as he had when he was discovered to have broken the decree. Analogous to the three who were thrown into the fiery furnace, words were lifted to Heaven as the wind carried them to the hearing of God. Those words came from the heart of Daniel, asking to be saved from the jaws of death that were surrounding him. As the hours of the night faded, one by one, Daniel was in the midst of animals that had been created to kill. In a place where death was a poisonous fragrance that carried throughout the air and filled his lungs, Daniel did not waver. Imagine standing in a place where death is absolute, and every minute that passes could be your last. He was starting to notice the lions were not attacking him. In a place where he was thrown to be the main course, satisfaction to the famished appetites of lions, it was as if they did not hunger for what had been served to them. In a place where chaos was expected, there was peace. In a place where death was expected, he still had life. God kept Daniel safe in a place of certain death, and he endured the night until he was freed by the king.

There is something that I want to show you in regard to both of the occurrences in biblical history that you may not have noticed at first glance. Our immediate attention is taken to the points of survival. How could it not be, as they all survived things that were instruments of death, things that no one was expected to live through? However, what I love about both encounters are the testimonies that followed. Both kings who had sentenced these mighty men of God to death had seen the glory of God. They both testified to the truth that God is real! They both acknowledged God because they could not explain or fathom within their human minds how these men had survived. This is a sure sign that something is from God, or that He has intervened in your situation. If your mind cannot fathom the outcome, nor can you explain intellectually what has taken place, it is from God. Our human minds cannot comprehend the fullness of God. So I want to encourage you, for the season of life that you are in, no matter what the battle may look like or what enemy is against you, not only will God give you victory but He will turn your battle into a testimony. You won't have to share this testimony, because everyone in your life will have front-row seats to God's glory. Others will speak of your testimony for you, because they will remember the battles you have faced. They will remember the scars you have displayed as proof of the fights that you have been in. Once they see you are victorious in this area of your life, they will say, "This had to be God." So never retreat, and never surrender. The Lord goes before you and fights for you. He has brought you too far to not see you through where He has brought you to. God is with you, mighty hero and mighty child of God!

Don't you realize that your body is the temple of the Holy Spirit, who lives in you and was given to you by God? You do not belong to yourself, for God bought you with a high price. So you must honor God with your body.

—1 Corinthians 6:19–20 (NLT)

CHAPTER 6

Taking Back Territory

The first thing we need to understand is that we do not belong to ourselves. Our bodies are temples of the Holy Spirit. Once you accept Jesus Christ into your life as Lord and Savior, the Holy Spirit makes His home within you. With that being said, your body is the territory of God's Holy Spirit, and it no longer belongs to the enemy. In order to protect yourself from the spiritual battle against the enemy, you must remain vigilant and watchful. In the garden of Gethsemane, Jesus instructed the apostles to keep watch and pray to protect themselves from temptation (Matthew 26:41 [NLT]). The statement that followed this direction from Jesus helps us understand why we need to keep watch and pray. Jesus proceeded to say, "The spirit is willing but the body is weak." Once we are redeemed by Jesus Christ and are now new creations through Him, our spirits are saved but our flesh is not. Our flesh remains carnal, which means there will still be carnal desires by our flesh. Our sinful nature will remain present as a constant adversary. The Holy Spirit empowers us to take dominion over our sinful nature. Temptations will still come, but you cannot open the gate to your heart and allow those temptations to overrun you. Once you have regained the territory the enemy had stolen, you have to learn from the losses along the way. Continue to update your battle plan (spiritual assessment and/or checklist from chapter 2) with strategies to help you

> **Temptations will still come, but you cannot open the gate to your heart and allow those temptations to overrun you.**

fortify the barriers in your life so that you are no longer vulnerable to the attacks you fell victim to. Ensuring that your battle plan is constantly updated with new information in regard to weak or vulnerable areas in your life will help you protect those areas. Therefore, submit those areas to God, and refresh your battle plan.

Your body is to be no longer used as an instrument of sin but to be a pure vessel to be used for the glory of God. That means you must guard every single part of your body that sin can enter and/or be used by the enemy. The apostle Paul wrote in the book of Romans, "Do not let any part of your body become an instrument of evil to serve sin. Instead, give yourselves completely to God, for you were dead, but now you have new life. So use your whole body as an instrument to do what is right for the glory of God" (Romans 6:13 [NLT]). Our bodies can either be used as vessels to do God's will or as instruments of sin. So let's address the different parts of our bodies that can be used as instruments of sin:

- Eyes
- Ears (in regard to hearing and listening)

- Mouth (specifically the tongue)
- Feet (walking in the direction of sin)
- Genitals (in regard to sexual sin and adultery)

Eyes

Let us start with the eyes, because I firmly believe this is where the craving of sin begins. I will use myself as an example. As you may have discovered by now, the adversary I faced on the battlefield of spiritual warfare was sexual sin. If I allowed my eyes to rest upon another woman and/or image, my flesh would be triggered. If I filled my line of sight with lustful images, they would be used as weapons of temptation against me. There was no secret that I was placing myself in a battle during this time. My mind would receive a sinful download of all that I allowed my line of sight to capture. This is why pornography is a paralyzing, addictive sin for many. It is the plan B of fulfilling a sinful fantasy. If I could not have the woman I desired, pornography would fulfill a fantasy by giving me a close-enough substitute. Once I married my spouse, this substitute became an excuse. I would use this sinful substitute for justification as it was helping me remain free of adultery. But, in reality, I was committing adultery the entire time. For Jesus says, in the Sermon on the Mount, "Those who look upon a woman lustfully has already committed adultery within his heart" (Matthew 5:28 [NLT]). Watching pornographic images on a screen was committing lustful sins with my eyes. I was committing adultery by allowing my eyes to rest upon those detestable images.

In order to break this cycle, I had to allow my eyes to rest upon things that were pleasing to God, and things that reminded me of Him and His goodness. I will provide you with some examples:

- The Bible (most important)
- Online ministries (church services)
- Christian YouTube ministries (*The Basement with Tim Ross*, *With the Perrys*, Ruslan KD, *Fighting for the Faith*, and *THE BEAT with Allen Parr*)
- Christian shows/movies (*The Chosen*, *Genesis: Paradise Lost*, and Christian documentaries)

These are just a few examples of how to ensure your eyes are resting upon things that lead you to God. First, renew and rewire your mind with God's Word. Allow the truth of what He speaks about the issue you are struggling with to penetrate your heart and transform your mind. Allowing God to change your mind is a very important step in your separation from this sin. Because, when He changes your mind, your heart will reflect what you think about this certain sin. Instead of watching secular shows that could trigger your flesh, watch shows that will direct your focus toward Jesus. It was in those times when I found myself consumed with boredom, and with an electronic device in my hand, that I was looking at things I should not have been looking at.

Therefore, the takeaway from this is, firstly, I found out that boredom was the initial emotion that would lead me to this path. Secondly, I needed to find healthier alternatives to entertain myself. So, instead of going directly to social media platforms (Instagram, Facebook, Reddit, or Twitter), I could go to the YouVersion Bible app instead. Because, if we are honest, most of these social media platforms have become pornographic websites (especially Reddit and Twitter). Also, influencers use Instagram as a platform for flesh. What I mean by that is that they will show more of their bodies to gain more attention. Stay away from soft-porn Instagram profiles. Unfollow that person who no longer leaves their body as a mystery but displays it as a tool for analytics. Because every follow, heart, and like medicates their pride.

For you, guarding your eyes could mean that you no longer watch the shows that you once watched. It could also mean you may need to take some time away from social media. I would rather walk away from social media or my favorite television shows than to walk away from God.

Ears (Hearing and Listening)

What are you allowing to enter your mind through the corridors of your ears? What or who are you listening to? What you hear or listen to can chart the direction in which you will go in that moment. If we are honest with ourselves, some of the things that consume our hearing are intoxicating to our flesh. For example, let us address the sin of gossip. The book of Proverbs, repetitively addresses gossip. I will give you a few Scriptures below:

> A troublemaker plants seeds of strife;
> gossip separates the best of friends.
>
> **—Proverb 16:28 (NLT)**
>
> Wrongdoers eagerly listen to gossip;
> liars pay close attention to slander.
>
> **—Proverb 17:4 (NLT)**
>
> As surely as a north wind brings rain,
> so a gossiping tongue causes anger!
>
> **—Proverb 25:23 (NLT)**

Based on our observation of the Scriptures that are listed above, we can clearly see a couple of things that are not fruitful for our walk of faith. In all three Scriptures, we see that gossip is represented in a negative way. Based on the three Scriptures above, gossip:

- Brings division
- Is eagerly partaken in by those with impure motives
- Causes anger

We can see the tangible evidence of what gossip can do, but why do people still partake in it? A conversation that is centered around gossip has the ability to draw people in and rob them of their attention. The gossip that you partake in can be a battle that you find yourself in, even moments after. For example, what if you wander into a conversation that leads to gossip about a particular issue that you struggle with and/or is triggering to you? Listening intently to conversations that are not Godly can be the ambush that was planted by the enemy. Remember, the enemy will launch sneak attacks against you, and he will use everything he can against you.

Gossip is a story about a person who is not present. It is, in most cases, fabricated and exaggerated. Firstly, it isolates the person who the story is about from the group. Secondly, it tells a tale of false information (in most cases) from a third-party source with minimal information, a sinful narrator who spreads slander about a person's misfortunes in order to paint a picture that stains the antagonist of the story. What if you were the person the story was about? I am sure that we all at some point in our lives have been the antagonists of someone's gossip. I am sure that we were the source of entertainment for people who wished to fill their time discussing our shortcomings or misfortunes. Do you remember what it felt like once you were enlightened about the words that were spoken about and against you? As followers of Christ, we are not to rejoice in the shame, sorrow, and pain of others. We are not to find entertainment in the struggles of others. Therefore, we cannot allow our ears to become the refuge for the detestable and fabricated lies that are birthed from sin. Do not allow the sounds of what seems as sweet as honey to be the poison that enters your hearing. Because what your ears welcome in will rest in your mind.

Mouth (Specifically the Tongue)

The tongue is a dangerous weapon that is armed with words that can be slanderous, painful, or false to hide one's true motives. For the words that rest upon the tongue can conceal the impure motives within the heart. A person can look you in the eyes and tell you the sweetest lie that will lead you to a destructive path. The tongue—and the words that flow from it—are the primary weapons for false prophets and/or teachers. I will provide you Scriptures from the book of Jerimiah to confirm this point:

> Then the Lord said, "These prophets are telling lies in my name. I did not send them or tell them to speak. I did not give them any messages. They prophesy of visions and revelations they have never seen or heard. They speak foolishness made up in their own lying hearts."
>
> **—JEREMIAH 14:14 (NLT)**

> This is what the Lord of Heaven's Armies says to his people: "Do not listen to these prophets when they prophesy to you, filling you with futile hopes. They are making up everything they say. They do not speak for the Lord!"
>
> **—JEREMIAH 23:16 (NLT)**

A manipulative person will use their words against you to control you. This is one way the enemy will try to detach you from God, by sending you in a direction that He did not send you in. We have to be able to use discernment to prevent ourselves from receiving lies that sound as if they are truth. Because a person who is a gifted liar and manipulator has mastered this weapon. Your vulnerability is their number one target. A person who operates in this way will recon your weaknesses and vulnerabilities to build a battle plan against you. Their manifesto of lies that are orchestrated as a recipe of destruction will be disguised as a symphonic song to address your vulnerability.

The spiritual warfare that we engage in is fought in the unseen world (spiritual realm), but people who are around you can be used as weapons in the seen world (physical realm). We also have to ensure that we are not being used as weapons against those who are around us. We cannot allow our own tongues to shoot fiery arrows of anger, condemnation, slander, and lies. If there is one thing I am certain of, it is this: the enemy comes to pervert and divide. The battlefield may be in your own home. The words that leave your mouth may be deadly weapons used against your family to inflict wounds of rejection, unworthiness, and verbal abuse that create an identity housed in self-consciousness. Verbal abuse within the home can have long-lasting consequences on a child or spouse. Verbal abuse that has become so damaging, from a voice that reaches higher decibels, causes the victim's body to react as if they are being physically attacked. A shout becomes a trigger and a weapon that deals a damaging blow to those we claim to love. The words that we speak should be words that promote love, healing, and peace, and leads the listener to Jesus Christ. For God is love (1 John 4:8 [NLT]), and the words that we speak should be representations of the love that God has for us.

Feet (Walking in the Direction of Sin)

Our feet are the instruments that carry us in the direction that points to the desires of our hearts. Your heart can be the driver behind the wheel, and your feet is the vehicle that transports you in whichever direction your heart sends you. When something enters your heart, you begin to crave it. There is a heightened desire for it, and you will pursue the desires of your heart without regard to the consequences. I remember there was a time in my life when I was twenty years old, and I did not have a vehicle.

There was this girl whom I had so much lust in my heart for during that time. She lived about a twenty to thirty minutes from me by foot, depending on the time of day or night. The lust within my heart for her was so strong, that I would literally walk to her house no matter the time of day. I can remember walking to her house in the middle of the night on multiple occasions. I had no regard for my safety because I could not see past my heart's desires. I did not have a vehicle at this time, so my feet where the vehicle that traversed down the path of fornication. Gratifying my flesh and satisfying its cravings made the walk feel like it was worth it. Because I was fulfilling my sinful needs, I don't ever remember having a single regret on any occasion in which I would travel to and from her house. This was because I was allowing my desire to fornicate to the light the path that was before me. This illuminated path of premarital sex and fornication became a beacon within the darkness that guided me to her bed. My heart wanted it, and my feet took me to it.

We cannot allow our sinful nature and it's cravings to be what fills our hearts. Nor can we allow them to light our path in which we walk throughout this life. We have to allow the Word of God to fill our hearts so that it is Him we pursue, and not sin. The book of Psalms tells us, "Your word is a lamp to guide my feet and a light for my path" (Psalm 119:105 [NLT]). The Word of God guides us, and it lights the path that is before us. It prevents us from moving in haste, and it keeps in pace with the timing of God. When you think of a lamp that you carry while walking down a dark path, the light does not travel far ahead of you. There is just enough light to see what is immediately surrounding you, and it can provide eight to ten feet of light before you. Therefore, you cannot move in haste, but you must walk carefully in order to protect yourself from unseen danger. Sin causes us to move in any direction, regardless of what is before us or around us. We move at an accelerated pace because our carnal appetite has to be satisfied in the moment. During those long walks, I was not walking with a lighted path but a darkened one. I was not walking in the way that would have been pleasing to God. I was walking a path that pleased only me. The lesson is this: do not stray away from the path that God's Word directs you to. For it is His perfect Word that lights the path that leads to eternal life, and not our sinful desires.

Genitals (In Regard to Sexual Sin and Adultery)

My eyes were the instruments that captured lustful images that sowed seeds of lust within my mind. My ears were the instruments that captured the sound of a woman's yes that opened the door to fornication and adultery. My tongue was the instrument that spoke deceitful words to provide a false illusion of love, when it was only lust. My feet were instruments that took me in the direction to fulfill my sinful desire. My genitals became tools to be utilized to commit sexual sin. The apostle Paul instructs us in the book of Romans to not allow our bodies to become instruments of sin (Romans 6:13 [NLT]). We saw this Scripture referenced earlier in this chapter. It was clearly a reference that I did not follow in the past. I allowed every part of me to become an instrument used for sin. Instead of walking in purity, I was drowning in a cesspool of lust. I was not saving the part of me that should have been preserved for my marriage night. I did not place my purity on a pedestal but used it as a form of surf and turf, easily accessible for any woman who had an appetite for it. I pawned my purity, and the return for it was damaging. I experienced an emptiness that could not be filled. No number of women could fill the void that was within me. So I went to pornography and used it as an alternate antibiotic to medicate the emptiness inside me. Masturbation provided a quick fix that would have to be replenished every day. It was an unaffordable therapy session that was costing me more than I was willing to pay. It cost me the way that I viewed and respected women.

I began to see women as prescriptions that I needed to medicate myself with. It was an over-the-counter solution that provided a quick remedy but did not properly address the sickness that was within me. Something had to change. No matter how hard the battle would be, I had to fight. What I mean by fight is that I had to be very real with myself and honest with God. I had to give Him my complete honesty, which was that my flesh loved the sins that I was committing, but I no longer wanted to live that way. I wanted to break free of the chains and be able to breathe freely. I no longer wanted to be suffocated by shame because of the life I chose to live. The answer was, and will always be, Jesus Christ. He sacrificed Himself to save me from spiritual death. His sacrifice created a pathway to the Father, something I did not have on earth. God constantly reminds me that He is, and always will be, a Father to me. I ran to the arms of my Savior, and through His grace and mercy, I am living a life that I once thought was unattainable. It was as if I had been standing on one side of a massive body of water, and the bridge to the other side had collapsed. In those moments of desperation, I cried out to my Savior, and Jesus rescued me every single time. So do not use yourself as an instrument for sin, but place yourself in the hands of God so that you can be used as an instrument of service and worship, an instrument for His glory and to serve His people. You, my friend, have a résumé; remember that. You have a relatable story that needs to be heard by others who are struggling with what you have struggled with. You have a powerful testimony. So allow God to use it, and you will change the lives of those He places in your path.

Even when I walk through the darkest valley, I will not be afraid, for you are close beside me. Your rod and your staff protect and comfort me.

—Psalm 23:4 (NLT)

CHAPTER 7

Facing Your Giants

At some point in our lives—whether past, present, or future—there will be a giant in the valley calling out to us, taunting us with our traumatic memories that are used against us as weapons to inflict some sort of spiritual PTSD (post-traumatic stress syndrome). This is not a malicious comment against those who do suffer from PTSD, but I want you to see the parallel here. Let us first venture into this topic from a biblical perspective. When there is a giant blocking your path to purpose, freedom, or healing, fear is the emotion that extinguishes the courage that is within you. In the book of 1 Samuel chapter 17, the Philistine champion Goliath taunted the army of Israel for forty days. The sound of his voice echoed from the valley as the wind provided natural acoustics to carry his voice throughout the Israelite camp. Each day, he pleaded for an opponent who would face him in this valley. The bargain made by the blasphemous giant was this: there would be a one-on-one, winner-takes-all battle. The army of the losing champion, so to speak, would become the slaves of the army the winner represented. However, for forty days, no one dared to enter the valley to face him. The fear that inflicted each and every soldier paralyzed their willingness to fight. Their weapons now felt heavier than ever before. Their armor did not feel as if it could provide adequate protection anymore. Their shields that had once protected them now seemed thin sheets of vulnerable material.

This is what fear does to those who are unwilling to face it. Fear is an emotion that foretells of events that do not exist or may never happen. Fear provides you with false predictions of the worst possible outcomes. Fear does not prophesy success or victory. It deceives you into believing you cannot overcome what is before you. It sinks you into a pit of deception and disbelief that transforms something that does not exist into a mirage or a false reality. Now your mind is processing the lies that fear has created into this false reality.

> **Fear is an emotion that foretells of events that do not exist or may never happen.**

Therefore, as every soldier looked into the valley, they did not see a chance of victory. They only saw certain defeat and inevitable death. The giant stood in their way of victory. As one day transitioned into another, they allowed victory to elude them. Like a thief who has stolen their desire to battle their oppressors, fear captured their courage. The adversary of fear conquered the army of Israel day after day. Goliath had not performed a single strike, nor had he done anything to warrant the fear that was inflicted upon the army. It was his appearance that extinguished the fire that once existed inside each of the soldiers. It wasn't until David arrived that someone was willing to go to battle with the giant. David entered the dark valley in the name of the Lord. Armed with only a shepherd's staff, a sling, and a rock, he conquered Goliath (1 Samuel 17:32–50 [NLT]).

What is the giant that calls out to you in your darkest moments? What does the voice of this giant say as its taunts echo throughout your mind? I remember the giant that was addiction, which became the walls of Jericho within my life. It was an impenetrable force that I did not believe I would ever conquer. I knew that, in order to conquer this giant, I had to face it. I had to go into the valley that had become a familiar place to me. There were times in my life when I thought I'd conquered the giant. However, one misstep or miscalculation, and I would find myself falling deep into the valley of relapse. A valley is a place that is created by the destruction between two mountains. Relapse was a place of destruction for me. In the depths of the valley, there were two things that I would notice:

1. How far I had fallen.
2. The great ascent that was before me.

This was a very dangerous place for me, spiritually and emotionally. The danger of being in this position is firstly, you've seen how far you have fallen. Secondly, you do not believe you have the strength or the fight left in you to ascend to freedom. This is when the lies begin to flow through your mind in waves of fear and despair, echoing statements such as, *Why am I even trying?* Or, *I will never defeat this.* Let me give you an analogy of shame and guilt that you may be able to relate to. Imagine you are in the depths of the ocean, and you begin to sink slowly. While you're sinking, your eyes are fixed on the surface of the water. As you are sinking, the surface becomes farther and farther away. The reflection of light that is given by the sun begins to slowly fade away, and now you have sunk to the ocean floor. Sitting in this abyss, with your eyes fixed in the direction of the surface, you feel this weight keeping you down. Knowing the distance to reach the surface is great, you begin to question if it is even worth the attempt to ascend. Feeling the full weight of guilt, you question if it would be better to just drown in this abyss and accept what you believe is inevitable. Shame sinks you, and guilt traps you. Guilt traps you with the fear of an unknown or false outcome. Fear is not a singular adversary; it comes with allies, operating in accord as a unified force to kill the purpose that God placed on you.

In order to overcome this great ascent, you have to learn from your mistakes. There is one thing I know for certain: the enemy constantly learns from our mistakes. Therefore, we must learn from them as well. So I began to analyze my approach to the giant of my life that was blocking my freedom. I began to notice:

1. I was attacking the issue head-on instead of seeking the source of the issue.
2. I was going into battle on my own strength.
3. I was fighting alone, when God had surrounded me with allies.
4. I was trying to utilize my own self-control instead of relying on the Holy Spirit.

I learned a valuable lesson from David that altered my approach. I could no longer go into this valley on my own strength to joust with what I perceived to be an unbeatable adversary. I had to lean into the strength of the Lord and allow Him to fight the battle for me. Therefore, I had to enter into the war room with a battle plan. One thing was certain: I had to get to the root cause of the issue. Most of the issues we face in life are not the source but the medication we run to to soothe the wound. So, with that being said, let us walk the path of addressing the roots.

Addressing the Roots

I discovered that pornography and promiscuity were the medications for the issues but were not the issues themselves. I sought refuge in sexual sin because of the issues of rejection and isolation I had faced throughout my life. I had been rejected during my exodus from the womb. My biological father had abandoned my mother and me while she was in labor with me. He did not show up to the hospital as a father would be expected to. He did not show up with a sense of pride to see that his legacy will be carried on in the tangible proof of another generation that shared his DNA. There were no words of affirmation or acceptance. There were no words that entered the atmosphere declaring his son was born. There were no shouts of joy that would echo throughout the corridors of the hospital. There was silence, as his absence was both physical and verbal. There were no words of acceptance, pride, or rejoicing that his firstborn son had arrived. I was left alone, unclaimed by a father, born to a young twenty-year-old mother. I did not understand how this would be the deepest root that would affect me for the majority of my life. So, there I was, a biracial child transiting through life. I didn't know where I fully belonged, since I am half African American and half Caucasian. I do not resemble either side, and I felt that my life had been a constant gray area, a prison of ambiguity with no door to the freedom of clarity. I was trapped between two sides because I could never fully fit into either one. I did not have a relationship with my father or his side of the family. So I did know how to accept that part of me. If I am being honest, I think I still don't understand that side of me. However, by the grace of God, I am moving in the right direction.

I remember this encounter that I had with a Caucasian female in high school. It may be able to provide clarity on what I mentioned in the paragraph above. This female (who I will not name) and I were attracted to each other. I pursued her, and I know that she was interested in me, but there was one statement she made that crushed me internally. This statement comes back to my memory from time to time, even to this day. She would write letters to me in my notebook to express her attraction, and I would do the same toward her. I asked her why we didn't just make it official since there was an obvious attraction. Her response was, "If I could paint you to be fully white, I would." As if my pigmentation could be altered like a filter placed on a photograph. I found myself explaining to her and reminding her that I am half Caucasian. It was obvious to me that "half" was not good enough. Was this a statement that rested in her heart, or was this a statement that had been taught to her by her family? After all, I did grow up in the Deep South. Nevertheless, I had once again felt the sting of rejection. I had been rejected by someone who said they liked me, and the dagger to my heart was that I am not fully Caucasian. This resembled the wound or the root of my birth but was not as deep. Someone who should have loved me had rejected me because they could not take me home to their family. I lived the majority of my life traversing this path of isolation, desperately wanting to belong somewhere with someone. I was broken; as a matter of fact, I still am. It is Jesus Christ who makes me whole. Apart from Him, I am that same broken child/teenager who felt isolated from the world.

This is why pornography is so dangerous to a person who deals with rejection. Pornography is a mirage of perversive fantasies of people who are never rejected. This is what is so enticing about it to people who have deep wounds of rejection. When you view pornography, you are viewing images of people who are paid to say yes. However, that is not the poisonous optics that is provided to your line of sight. The actors (if you can call them that) are not rejecting any advances or requests for the other. So, for people who have dealt with constant rejection, this is intoxicating. Not only do you get to see people *not* be rejected, but you get to fulfill any fantasy you have. This is a trap and a sickness that digs its claws deep inside of you. The people who are on the other side of that camera are just as broken as we are. Exposing yourself to media devices shared by millions of people is a degrading thing to do. These "actors" are selling off their dignity and pawning off their purity. When you pawn something, you never receive the full value for it. The pawnshop owner's number one priority is profit. He or she will pay you as low as they can for what you are pawning, and then they will sell it for a higher price. This is how that industry operates. It will pay the people who participate a lesser value than they are worth, and it will maximize their profit using their bodies and their wounds as currency. We cannot be consumers of something that damages us even further. It does not heal the wounds that are on the inside of us. It just creates more root issues that we will have to address. Therefore, we have to get to the root issues and see beyond the medications we are using. We are committing malpractice upon ourselves by seeking out ways to heal that only cause more damage. In order to slay this giant that was before me, I had to change my perspective.

Change Your Perspective of Your Giant

I will give you an acronym for "giant" to help you anchor in Jesus:

- **G**od
- **I**s
- **A**lways
- **N**ear
- **T**o
- **S**ave

No matter what your giant is—whether it is alcoholism, addiction, or feeling like you just don't know where you fit in—remember that God is always near to save you. He is never far, nor will He ever leave you. Knowing that God is near gives us the confidence we need to face the giants that are in our lives. In the book of Deuteronomy it says, "Do not be afraid or discouraged, for the Lord will personally go ahead of you. He will be with you; he will neither fail you nor abandon you" (Deuteronomy 31:8 [NLT]). Let us rest right here for a moment. The Lord will "personally" go ahead of you, and He will be with you. This speaks to us an assurance that, no matter what is before us, God is there. It also speaks to us that we are not alone during our progression toward the unknown. God has me covered for the things that I do not see, and He is with me through all of my present storms in life. In lives where so many of us have been abandoned and rejected, the second part of verse 8 tells us, "He will neither fail you nor abandon you." We may have been rejected by family, friends, or people we thought had finally accepted us. None of that matters, because I serve a God that will never fail me and will never abandon me. When my earthly father rejected me, my heavenly Father accepted me. When my earthly father abandoned me, my heavenly Father was always with me. I can now uproot the roots that had been hidden beneath the surface of wounds, and I can cut down this poisonous tree. I know that God accepts me, affirms me, and will never leave me. Whatever the giant may be in your life, lean into God so that He can help you slay your giant, just as He did for me.

Do not be afraid or discouraged, for the Lord will personally go ahead of you. He will be with you; he will neither fail you nor abandon you.

—Deuteronomy 31:8 (NLT)

CHAPTER 8

The Battle Is the Lord's

The first step in preparing for a battle is understanding that it is not yours to fight. You may be the vessel that will carry out the act in some cases. However, it is the Lord's battle, and victory is found in the name of Jesus. The hardest thing for some of us to do is to get out of our own way. We have become our own barriers and obstacles in the battles we face. We refuse to loosen our grip on things that we cannot control. Therefore, we accept defeat in these areas of our lives because pride deceives us into thinking that we are the be-all and end-all. If the battle begins and ends with us, defeat is certain. The enemy lines that we may find ourselves behind are the battles we are fighting against ourselves. We each have become our own worst enemy that inflicts internal wounds upon ourselves. Our shortcomings pierce our will to fight, like the strongest and sharpest steel that is deadly to the touch. This sword of failure impales our faith to continue moving forward because success does not seem certain. The enemy wishes to trade the full armor of God that we are outfitted with for armor that increases our vulnerability. The enemy wants you to trade the belt of truth for the belt of lies. Every piece of the armor of God is connected to the belt of truth. Therefore, if the enemy can deceive you into believing that you have forfeited your salvation, you will not have faith for the other components. If you do not believe the truth that you are saved by grace by placing your faith in Jesus, then you will not wear the helmet of salvation. This is why we must allow the Lord to fight the battles for us. The epigraph for this chapter gives us a blueprint for how to get out of our own way.

There are some battles in our lives that we will not give to the Lord because we don't want to face them. We place them into the deep abyss of our subconsciousness to be locked deep inside of us so that we will never have to face them. Our hardest battles are the ones that we never face. We never face them because fear has decimated our faith and belief that we can be healed and/or free of this. We are in bondage to unfought battles. The Lord tells us, "Do not be afraid or discouraged." This means we no longer have to hide in fear from our battles. We no longer have to be filled with discouragement because God fights for us. I know that you may have taken losses, and you may have failed many times. I want to remind you that, no matter how many times you have fallen, the battle is not over. I know there are seasons of our lives that seem so dark, chaotic, and unwinnable. In these moments, we have to remember the Lord is near and never far. We no longer have to be afraid to bring our deepest internal battles to light. The Lord knows every struggle, thought, and wound that you have. No matter how deep you try to bury it, He still knows it is there. I know that you may have tried everything, and none of it has seemed to work, but God is with you. "He is near to the brokenhearted, and he rescues those whose spirits are crushed" (Psalm 34:18 [NLT]). He is there when it feels as if your heart has been shattered, and He will rescue you. Just let it go, and release it to God. Give Him the battle that He wants to fight for you.

During the Sermon on the Mount, Jesus said, "Blessed are the poor in spirit, for theirs is the Kingdom of Heaven" (Matthew 5:3 [New King James Version]). The New Living Translation provides a clearer context, and it says, "God blesses those who are poor and realize their need for Him, for the Kingdom of Heaven is theirs" (Matthew 5:3 [NLT]). In the first line of the beatitudes, Jesus says that God blesses those who realize their need for Him. This is a calling to become totally reliant on God. When we enter into the refuge of our Heavenly Father, there is no longer a need to fear the unknown of a future that has not yet come. Nor should we concern ourselves with our current situations. When fear and discouragement creep into the corridors of our minds, they release the toxins of stress within us. Stress has the ability to bring forth a metamorphic change in our emotions that transforms confidence into fear. These two weights that keep us in deep and dark places are intertwined. Each contributes to the other, as stress brings forth fear. The more stressed we feel about a certain situation, the more fearful we can become of it. The more fearful we become, the more stressed we become. The words and teachings of Jesus Christ lead us into an opposite direction, away from the things that cause us fear and discouragement. He invites us to come and find rest in Him, and to take His yoke upon us. For His light and His burden are easy. When we fully rely on God, we can have victory in the areas of our lives that once brought fear and discouragement.

Have you ever found yourself feeling fearful or discouraged about something God was calling you to? As if the résumé that is your life had indefinitely disqualified you from the area He was calling you to. When we analyze our lives through our limited perspectives, I'm sure there are things we feel as if we should not be doing. If God has called you to ministry, you may feel your life has disqualified you from being a shepherd of God's flock. When the battles within your mind begin, the enemy wants to deceive you into believing that you are more of a hypocrite than a shepherd, that every word that comes from your mouth is a word that is different than the life you are living. I know this battle all too well. I received the call to ministry two months after I submitted my life to Jesus Christ. There were a lot of issues I was learning to navigate, and there was still flesh that had to be crucified. So, when I received the call, there was a decision to be made. *Do I answer the call, or do I keep God on hold? Do I send God to voicemail because I feel undeserving of this call?* Ministry was not something that I had ever desired, but I wanted to obey God. I didn't know how or where to even begin, as I am a first-generation pastor in my family. I answered the call and stepped out in faith. God opened a door for me to begin to develop in ministry, and I would preach one or two services a month. I remember, after my first sermon, before I left the podium, I whispered to myself, "God, I hope I brought you glory." I immediately began to question myself before I departed the stage and arrived at my seat. What I did not realize in that moment was that I had opened the door for a battle with the enemy.

I had given him an open door to walk in and bring forth spiritual warfare. I opened myself up to an ambush by placing my focus on all the reasons why I believed that I should not be in ministry. As soon as I sat down in my car, the enemy began to tell me how bad my sermon was. He began to attack the calling that God had placed on my life. There was a constant barrage of attacks against my knowledge of the Bible and my public speaking. It was time for another decision to be made, and I could not rest in that defeated position. I had to make the decision in that particular moment. I had to decide whether to believe I am who God says I am, or I am what the enemy says I am. The line in the sand had been drawn, and I would either continue in faith or accept defeat. I chose to believe that I am who God says I am. The Bible tells us the enemy is the father of lies, so if the origin of lies begins at his lips, why would I accept his opinion of me? The enemy's opinion of you is not the truth of who you are. The enemy's goal is to deceive you into aborting the purpose God has placed inside of you. So, when Joshua became the leader of the Israelites after the death of Moses, you can imagine how he possibly felt in that moment. I can imagine the thoughts that were traversing his mind, questioning how he could be what Moses was to the people. Joshua was present for all the things that God accomplished through Moses.

> **The enemy's goal is to deceive you into aborting the purpose God has placed inside of you.**

I am sure there could have been thoughts of intimidation and doubt, and feeling unqualified. God met Joshua in this moment of transition from being a follower to becoming a leader with a perfect response. Deuteronomy 31:8 was God's assurance to Joshua that He was with him. God was not asking Joshua to become Moses, nor did He need a duplicate of Moses. In this season, He needed a Joshua, for it was Joshua's assignment to lead the Israelites into the promised land. God informed Joshua with the assurance that He will never fail him nor abandon him.

This was a powerful reminder, as if God was saying, "I will be with you just as I was with Moses. Just because Moses is no longer present does not mean that I will no longer be present." Our God keeps His promises and covenants, and He promised to lead them to the land that He had promised to Abraham. He was reestablishing the covenant He had made to their forebearers, Abraham, Isaac, and Jacob. You are who God needs in this season. Just as God assured Joshua that He would be with him throughout all that was to come, He will be with you as well. God needs you, and not who you believe you need to be in order to serve Him. You do not have to transform into what you believe would best qualify you for what God has for you. Submit to the Holy Spirit, and He will qualify you with the gift(s) that you will need. It is through the power of the Holy Spirit that we become who God is calling us to be. We merge into the identity God created us to live when we no longer accept the lie of who the enemy says we are. The world needs *you* because no one can do what God has called you to do, in the way He created you to do it.

God will never fail you, nor will He ever abandon you.

It is time to release the battle that you've been fighting alone. I know you are tired, and it seems as if the hardships that you have been facing are never-ending. I know the battles that you have fought in silence have been unbearably heavy, like a weight that feels as if it has crushed every desire within you to press on. I know there have been times when you've wanted to give up. Throwing in the towel seemed as if it was the only path to peace. This is what it is like when we fight with our own strength. This is the outcome of fighting a battle that we are not anointed to fight.

There were seasons of my life when I struggled to remain pure and obedient to God. I remember crying out to God in utter confusion and bewilderment. I could not figure out in the moment why I could not receive victory in those vulnerable areas of my life. During those seasons, I felt isolated and alone. It felt as if God was a great distance from me. I could not understand how God felt so distant, and I continued to stumble and fall short. The Lord revealed to me that I cannot have victory when I am doing all of the fighting. I was seeing the battle through the results of my own efforts without realizing that my efforts alone wouldn't get me anywhere. I was going against an army with guerilla warfare tactics, instead of allowing God to be the general of the battle. I want to encourage you to surrender the battle to the Lord. Give Him every weight that you have been carrying, and have faith that He is with you. God is omnipresent, which means He is with you at all times. You may not feel Him or hear from Him audibly, but He is there. The even better news is that He will always be there, and He will never abandon you. For He is Jehovah Tsaba, which translates to "the Lord will fight for you." Give Him the battle, and I promise that you will begin to see victory where there was once defeat.

And they have defeated him by the blood of the Lamb and by their testimony. And they did not love their lives so much that they were afraid to die.

—Revelation 12:11 (NLT)

CHAPTER 9

The Blood of the Lamb

As believers in Jesus Christ, we are free because He shed His blood to atone for our sins. He fulfilled the requirement of the law by satisfying the penalty that our sins incurred. Jesus Christ was rightly referenced to as the "lamb of God who takes away the sins of the world" by John the Baptist (John 1:29 [NLT]). The blameless and spotless lamb entered the Jordan River to submit Himself to baptism. The moniker "lamb of God" was a reference to Mosaic law. During the time of Moses and the Israelites in the wilderness, God gave Moses instructions regarding the atonement of sin. In order for a person who has committed sin to be absolved, they had to sacrifice the firstborn male lamb. The lamb had to be spotless, without blemish. This parallels with being pure and untainted. So you can understand the reference as Jesus shed His blood to fulfill the requirement of the law, as He was blameless, spotless, and lived a life that we could not live, to pay the debt that we could not pay. However, this chapter's epigraph goes back into history a little further, prior to the exodus from Egypt, to be specific. The first fulfillment and manifestation of the epigraph was a night of death, a night in which, for those who did not have the blood of the lamb on their doorpost, death would enter and serve a deadly blow. The cost of not having the blood of the lamb was the firstborn son and the firstborn animal of that particular house. For those who did have the blood of the lamb on their doorpost (per the instructions given to Moses by God), death would pass over their home (Exodus 11:1–30 [NLT]).

I want to show you the importance here in regard to the spiritual warfare that we all face. As the death angel passed through the land, death arrived unnoticed. For, it says in Scripture, the Egyptians woke up during the night and found death where there was once life. There was not a single house in which an Egyptian did not die (Exodus 11:30 [NLT]). There were loud wailings of sorrow and pain that entered the atmosphere of Egypt. This was the notification to the Hebrew people that the death angel had passed through the land and served his purpose. So, because they were covered by the blood of the lamb, death had passed over them. As believers of Jesus Christ, we are covered by the blood of the lamb. This means there may have been seasons in your life when the enemy launched a barrage of attacks against you. However, none of those attacks came close to you because of the blood of Jesus that covers you. The blood of the lamb sealed the homes of the Hebrew people from death. The death angel saw blood, and he did not enter. He did not care who was on the other side of the door. He did not look for the Hebrew ethnicity; he looked for the blood of the lamb. The difference between life and death—Hebrew or Egyptian—on the night of the first Passover was the blood of a lamb.

This is why we can have peace during the storms of life and the battles that we may find ourselves in. The weapon may be formed, but it will not succeed. The blood of Jesus seals us and protects us as long as *we* keep the gates closed to sin. We have to be cautious to not place ourselves in self-inflicted battles. The blood of Jesus, and our testimony, serve two purposes:

1. They testify to the power of Jesus Christ.
2. They testify of what He brought us through, and they give hope to those who bear witness.

Our testimony is grown from the seeds of trials that were sown in the soil of adversity. The tests of life evolve to some of our greatest testimonies. Our testimonies are weapons that not only spark boldness and courage inside the hearts of believers in Jesus, but also provide hope to those who can only see the storm they are currently in. There is a transitional space between our tests and testimonies. The enemy's goal is to trap us in the transitions of life. Transitions prepare us for what awaits us after we depart our seasons of isolation and/or development.

There is always an assignment or mission from God on the other side of a wilderness. If the enemy can ensnare you in his traps of temptation in transition, you will not be a threat to take his territory. Let us take a look at this from a perspective of offense and defense in regard to a battle. We know that attacking a strong army during times of vulnerability increases the chances of success.

> **Our testimony is grown from the seeds of trials that were sown in the soil of adversity.**

Therefore, imagine your platoon is traveling on this narrow path (narrow is the gate and path that leads to eternal life (Matthew 7:13–14 [NLT])). The enemy has reconned your movements, and it is fully aware of your plans to transition from one location to the next. The enemy begins to create a battle plan against you. The enemy and his soldiers position themselves on each side of the narrow path, camouflaging themselves by taking cover in the surrounding trees and water. They watch intently as they wait for the perfect moment to strike. They patiently wait for the most vulnerable moment to attack. Once they see the opening and/or vulnerable posture they've been waiting for, they strike. It's an ambush! You're scrambling to regain a defensive and dominant position so that you can be postured to defend yourself. As you are attempting to retreat to higher ground in hopes of regrouping, you see the enemy blow through your platoon like a hurricane, wiping out all who were not watchful and vigilant. You find yourself to be in an unwinnable position, and the battle is lost.

The path and gate to enter into eternal life is narrow, and it is a difficult path to walk. The enemy and his soldiers are hidden along the path with traps of temptation set. If you do not remain watchful or vigilant, you will find yourself in the middle of an ambush by the enemy. This ambush could've been countered to place yourself in a winnable position if you had reconned the path that you were traversing. For example, if you find yourself in a location that triggers lustful or other sinful desires, it may be best to leave that location. Pride is a self-inflicted wound that is weaponized against us. We allow ourselves to remain in compromising places because we believe we can abstain from the desires on our own strength. For example, if I am feeling vulnerable, I may want to avoid the gym or other places where I may lustfully look upon women. Avoiding the gym in my moments of vulnerability helps me to remain vigilant and watchful. I am not placing myself in a position to walk into an ambush of temptation.

There will be days when you will have to be really honest with yourself. You will have to perform an honest self-check, and understand the places you should not visit during your vulnerable moments. If you are a technical thinker, you can develop some form of an action plan that measures your vulnerability and identifies places you may want to avoid. The most typically used method of measurement is a scale from one to ten. By using simple methods, you can begin to create self-awareness tools that will help you remain accountable to keep yourself in check. I will provide you with a short example on how this could potentially look. Again, you do not have to overcomplicate it. Make it as simple as possible, but tailor it to your specific situations and triggers.

Vulnerability Self-Check

Struggle	Vulnerability Level	Avoid	Contingency Plan
Sexual Sin	10	Gyms and Beaches	Exercise at Home
Anger	8	Crowded Areas	Pray and Read the Bible
Alcohol Addiction	9	Gatherings Near Bars	Accountability Partners
Anxiety/ Depression	8	Isolation	Meet with Community

The sample above is a working model that you can tailor to your specific needs. I encourage you to seek God and pray for His guidance to help you create this part of your battle plan. I have listed numerous examples that can be compiled into a battle plan for you. Creating practical weapons, such as the examples within this book, will help you become battle-ready! If you can properly identify the struggle, then you can seek God to identify the ambush.

The places that we are to avoid are the places in which we have fallen and/or have been trapped in temptation. I know creating tools such as this can sometimes make you feel like less of an adult. It almost feels childlike in a sense, but a child has little to no self-control. A child has to be properly guided in order to not place themselves in harmful positions. We, as parents, do our best to guide our children away from harmful situations to protect them. So these are tools that God can equip you with to ensure you are avoiding situations that harm you and your relationship with God. Remember, a sin such as sexual sin, is a sin against your own body. The apostle Paul wrote to the church in Corinth, "Run from sexual sin! No other sin so clearly affects the body as this one does. For sexual immorality is a sin against your own body" (1 Corinthians 6:18 [NLT]). Avoiding places that trigger sexual sin helps us prevent sinning against our own bodies (the temples of the Holy Spirit).

We are freed by the blood of the lamb and by the words of our testimonies. The word testimony in Hebrew is *aydooth*, which means "do it again with the same power and authority." Every time we speak out or read a testimony, we are asking the Lord to "do it again with the same power and authority." The word testimony in Greek is *martyias*, which comes from *martus*, or evidence given (judicially or in a genitive case), as in a record, report, testimony, and witness. When you testify, you are providing a statement that gives evidence of proof or fact. In regard to Christianity, it is considered to be a public recounting of a conversion or experience. So, when we look at the essence of what a testimony is, we see that it is a public recounting that provides evidence to what God has done for us.

Let me give you an example. About fourteen years ago, I was in a car accident. This was an accident that I should not have walked away from. I remember traveling down the highway, and the back tire on the driver's side of my car exploded. It felt as if the back of the car was elevated off the highway about two to three feet during the explosion. I remember the moment when I was losing control of the car, and it was as if time had slowed down. During this time, I looked to my left (because I was in the right lane of the highway), and I saw that my car was drifting toward the car to my left. During this slow-motion moment, I looked in the back seat, and I saw children. It was as if one of the children and I had made eye contact, and I knew I could not be the cause of this child being injured. So I made the decision that if something bad was going to happen, it would be to me and not to these children. I pulled the steering wheel to the right to veer clear of the car, and my car went off the highway and began to roll. On the initial impact of the first roll, I blacked out.

I remember I came to my senses and opened my eyes to find myself sitting on the roof of my car (I was not wearing a seat belt) as the car was upside down and was resting in about two feet of water. I found a way to exit the vehicle, and I navigated my way to the side of the highway where people were already sprinting toward my location. I didn't realize in the moment that I had just received a miracle. I did not feel any pain, nor did I have any visible injuries. I figured maybe when the adrenaline wore down, the pain would come in like a rushing flood. To my surprise, the parents who had been driving the car that was to my immediate left (the parents of the child I made eye contact with and had pulled my steering wheel to avoid) were among the first to arrive to my location. They informed me that they saw what I had done to avoid hitting their car, and they thanked me. I could see the emotion in the eyes of the mother as her voice trembled. This was a genuine reaction that I oddly was not expecting. I just knew that I did not want to be the cause of a child being hurt badly, and I had been willing to sacrifice myself so that would not happen. Sometime later, I was transported to the nearest hospital to be evaluated. I was hospitalized for about three days, but there were no present injuries. They could not find anything wrong with me. We were all bewildered as to how someone who was not wearing a seatbelt, and whose car had performed multiple rolls, did not have any injuries. How was this possible? Mind you, I was not a follower of Christ at this point. However, God protected me even during my time of rebellion. He knew that a moment was coming in which I would fully surrender my life to Him. God had a plan for my life before I even knew that I would submit to Him.

This is how my testimony and the blood of Jesus frees me. I can look back during this time (and many other occurrences), and say that it is only by God's grace that I am alive. I can give a public account and declare that I am a walking miracle. I could have taken my last breath on that day, but God had other plans. God did not allow that day to be my last day on earth. I have absolute faith in God for whatever I may encounter in this life. The same way that He protected me then, I know He can and will continue to do so. You have a testimony; we all do. There are times that I know you can retrospectively think back on and say it was only by God's grace that you made it through. Do not allow the lies of the enemy and the difficulties of life to silence your testimony. We are saved by the shed blood of the lamb of God. We testify to His goodness, and it is only through Him that we will have eternal life. That is the most important testimony! Jesus Christ lived a life that we could not live, and He paid a debt that we could not pay, because He was the only one who could do it! Our lives are living, breathing, and walking testimonies of this. I encourage you to declare your testimony boldly, as it is one of your greatest weapons against the enemy. It is the proof and evidence of God's faithfulness. Your testimony could be the fuel to ignite the faith of someone who is on the verge of giving up. Keep pressing on, my friend. God is with you!

So now there is no condemnation for those who belong to Christ Jesus. And because you belong to him, the power of the life-giving Spirit has freed you from the power of sin that leads to death.

—**Romans 8:1-2 (NLT)**

CHAPTER 10

Victory in the Name of Jesus

We know the word victory simply means that you have overcome an opponent. However, let us review an alternate definition of victory. According to *Merriam-Webster's Dictionary*:

> *Victory:* achievement of mastery or success in a struggle or endeavor against odds or difficulties.

Victory, in this context, means that you have mastered

a struggle in spite of the odds or resistance it brought. Throughout the journey we have embarked on through the corridors of each chapter in this book, I want to be clear on something: none of what you have read will help you, if you first do not understand that you already have victory through Jesus Christ. He is the foundation of our victory, because it is only achievable through Him.

Jesus Christ mastered a life that we could not master. He was successful in the atonement of our sins. He achieved all that He was sent to accomplish, regardless of the odds that were against Him and the resistance that He faced.

> **Victory is unattainable without the one who created the pathway for it.**

Victory is unattainable without the one who created the pathway for it. One of my favorite Scriptures that I have to anchor in recently is found in Psalms chapter 46. It reads, "Come, see the glorious works of the Lord: See how he brings destruction upon the world. He causes wars to end throughout the earth. He breaks the bow and snaps the spear; he burns the shields with fire. 'Be still, and know that I am God! I will be honored by every nation. I will be honored throughout the world.' The Lord of Heaven's Armies is here among us; the God of Israel is our fortress" (Psalm 46:8–11 [NLT]).

There is a portion of Scripture that I highlighted for you to focus on. In a world that is constantly moving and changing, it is easy to find ourselves being swept away by what seems to be a never-ending cycle of sin and repentance. We have become so overwhelmed with trying to resist temptation, live righteously, and fight the battle of spiritual warfare on our own. We are in a constant defensive posture, fighting off the resistance of temptation. Throughout this spiritual chaos, we forget that God tells us to "be still, and know that I am God!" The first thing He tells us to do is to "be still." He is telling us to surrender whatever it is that we are trying to do on our own, to give up our self-righteous crusade of fighting for our spiritual freedom alone, which is filled with pride. God is telling us to rest in Him, and allow Him to do the things that we cannot do on our own. When we refuse to be still and rest in Him, our actions tell a hard truth about our faith in God. Our actions speak a different language than what we believe.

- We are indirectly proclaiming with our actions that we do not trust that He can do what we can't do.
- We believe that we can win the battle and attain absolute victory without Him.
- We believe that we are sufficient enough to overcome any obstacle that is positioned before us.

This is a perfect segue into the second portion of the Scripture, which says, "Know that I am God." The complete context of this Scripture is to give God the totality of all that we are facing and/or struggling with. God is omniscient (all-knowing). He knows what has happened, is happening, and will happen in your life. Therefore, submit to Him all the things that you are battling that He already knows about. He is ready to fight for you, but you have to make the choice to submit and surrender it to Him. God is instructing us to remember who He is, for He is everything that we need, whenever we need Him to be it. He is the great "I Am"; He is Immanuel (God is with us). We see in the holy Scriptures that He is faithful, He keeps His promises, and He fights for us. The war that has been waged against you in your life has not escaped His sight. The prayers that you have prayed have not fallen on deaf ears; He has heard every single word.

God's Word tells us that in Exodus chapter 3. It reads, "Then the Lord told him, "I have certainly seen the oppression of my people in Egypt. I have heard their cries of distress because of their harsh slave drivers. Yes, I am aware of their suffering. So I have come down to rescue them from the power of the Egyptians and lead them out of Egypt into their own fertile and spacious land. It is a land flowing with milk and honey—the land where the Canaanites, Hittites, Amorites, Perizzites, Hivites, and Jebusites now live" (Exodus 3:7–8 [NLT]). Exodus chapter 3 will bring more truth to what we are discussing. In Exodus chapter 3, we see that God:

- Sees
- Hears
- Knows
- Moves

God saw the oppression the children of Israel endured during their bondage in Egypt. He heard their cries of distress and their calls for freedom. He was aware of all of the suffering they endured. God Himself came down to rescue the Hebrew people from Egypt with numerous plagues, and He sent Moses to lead their exodus from Egypt. This is how we can rest in God and be still. We know that He sees, hears, knows, and moves on our behalf. God sees the battles that you are fighting. He hears your cries of distress and every prayer that you have prayed. He knows the struggles and pain that you have endured. If you will be still, and have faith to believe that He is who His Word says that He is, He will move on your behalf. There is peace when you are still and in the presence of God. When you anchor into this verse, no matter what comes against you, it will not overwhelm you. You will be able to be still and allow God to have all control over the situation.

Our epigraph for this chapter is also important for us to receive victory through Jesus. The enemy constantly attacks our identities and our salvation. It is in those moments when you fall short that you can hear his deceitful voice. He moves in while you're wounded, to deceive you into believing that your identity is your mistakes. The enemy wants you to believe you are the mistakes that you make. If he can get you to absorb this false identity, he can trick you into believing that Jesus Christ has walked away from you. We have to remember that there is no condemnation for those who belong to Jesus Christ, but the enemy wants you to believe that you are condemned. In the aftermath of our mistakes, it is as if we are in an interrogation room. We have been momentarily captured as a prisoner of spiritual war. The enemy is interrogating us with hopes of deceiving us to confess that we are nothing more than the sin(s) that we fell into. Let us walk this out in an example.

The Interrogation Room "Behind Enemy Lines"

The enemy: I see that you fell into the trap we set for you by lusting after the woman who captured your vision. It started as glances, but I knew that if we positioned her in front of you in the right moment (in a vulnerable state where you were not vigilant), those glances would turn to stares. You are nothing more than an adulterer.

Chris: I am not my mistakes or the sins that I commit.

The enemy: You are indeed the mistakes you commit. You don't love Jesus as you say you do. Didn't Jesus say that "if you love Him, you would obey His commandments" (John 14:15 [NLT])? Didn't Jesus tell the people during the Sermon on the Mount "that if you look upon a woman lustfully, you have committed adultery in your heart" (Matthew 5:28 [NLT])?

Chris: God's holy Word also says, "If we claim we have no sin, we are only fooling ourselves and not living in the truth. But if we confess our sins to him, he is faithful and just to forgive us our sins and to cleanse us from all wickedness" (1 John 1:8–9 ([NLT]). Therefore, I lay my sins at the altar of grace. I confess my sins to Him, and I am forgiven, because His Word is truth! Jesus paid for all of my sins on the cross with His blood, and He atoned for my sins. My past, or present mistakes do not define me, because God is faithful to forgive me when I repent of my sins.

The enemy: You are nothing more than an addict. You will always be that broken child who I held captive in sin since you were a child.

Chris: I am no longer that broken child. Jesus Christ healed me from spiritual death. For the Word of God says, "But he was pierced for our rebellion, crushed for our sins. He was beaten so we could be whole. He was whipped so we could be healed" (Isaiah 53:5 [NLT]). I was healed from spiritual death and sin because of Jesus's sacrifice. I am no longer that broken child who was consumed by sin. I am a new creation by placing my faith in Jesus Christ that He died for my sins. The truth of God's Word tells me, "Therefore, if anyone is in Christ, he is a new creation. The old has passed away; behold, the new has come" (2 Corinthians 5:17 [NLT]).

The enemy: The life you live and the traps that you fall into disqualify you from the grace of God. You are not loved, nor will you ever be loved. You are weak, vulnerable, and will never overcome the sins of your past.

Chris: I may be weak and vulnerable apart from Christ; but with Him, I am more than a conqueror! (Romans 8:37 [NLT]). I am not a victim of my circumstances and a captive of my mistakes. I am not a casualty to my past, nor will I be oppressed by your lies! I may be weak, but God's grace is sufficient. For His holy Word says, "Each time he said, 'My grace is all you need. My power works best in weakness.' So now I am glad to boast about my weaknesses, so that the power of Christ can work through me. That's why I take pleasure in my weaknesses, and in the insults, hardships, persecutions, and troubles that I suffer for Christ. For when I am weak, then I am strong" (2 Corinthians 12:9–10 [NLT]).

[The enemy flees.]

We do not combat the lies of the enemy with our own intellect but with the Word of God. We combat lies with the truth of what God says about us. We testify to the sacrifice of Jesus Christ, and to His resurrection that broke the power of sin. The Gospel is not just a set of Scriptures; it is a person, and that person is Jesus Christ!

You have victory in Christ, for He won the battle through His death and resurrection. We cannot experience true victory outside of Jesus. True victory is only attained by surrendering to Him. Then we are able to allow His perfect power to strengthen our weaknesses and vulnerabilities. I am here to remind you again that you are:

- Not a victim to your circumstances.
- Not held captive by your mistakes.
- Not a casualty to your past.
- Not bound and oppressed by the lies of the enemy if you live through Christ!

We may not be able to rewrite the manuscript of our past, but we can change the narrative of the story that is before us. I believe there are times when we find ourselves caught in the past, attempting to rewrite what we cannot change. Our focus is anchored to the unchangeable narratives that are already molded in stone. Our past is an unchangeable history, but this history—no matter how bad it may be—can be used for good. Your history gives you a résumé that makes you credible to those who are drowning in what you have survived. My question to you is, how will you use the part of your life that you cannot change? Will you allow it to become a testimony of victory through Jesus Christ? Or will you allow it to continue to be deadweight that sinks you into a deep and dark abyss of discouragement? There is power in what you see as a part of the life you wish to no longer to remember. This is an area of your life where you believed you would never see victory.

It is time to fight for who you are becoming. It is time to go to war with the lies of the enemy with the truth of God's Word as your weapon. It is time to pick up your cross and follow Jesus, and not surrender to the temptations of this world. God gave you the breath of life and allowed you to see this day. This means He still has a purpose, plan, and future for you. There is still some fight left in you. What will this chapter of your life say about you? What will the story of the chapters to be written in the future say about you? If God is for you, it doesn't matter who or what is against you (Romans 8:31 [NLT]). I believe in you, and most importantly, God believes in you. I decree and declare by faith: the best part of your story is ahead of you. The words that will be written about you will be a testament to God's faithfulness and your perseverance. It is time to put on the full armor of God and get back in the fight. May the grace of the Lord be with you, as He goes before you and fights on your behalf.

What shall we say about such wonderful things as these? If God is for us, who can ever be against us?

—Romans 8:31 (NLT)

CONCLUSION

We have come to the end of our journey within the pages of this book. However, there will still be battles in this life to fight. I pray that all that is included in this book will help you in your walk of faith. I encourage you to pray to God, and seek His guidance on the assessments and checklists that I have included within this book. I believe these are practical steps that will help you remain vigilant and watchful on the path that leads to eternal life. You are ready for whatever the enemy will bring your way. It is time to suit up for battle and face the giants that are in your life. Victory is already in your possession, because you belong to the Savior who defeated sin and the enemy. The path ahead may be perilous, but the Savior calms every storm that may arise in your life. Follow the guidance of the Holy Spirit, and He will lead in all truth to the truth, way, and life. God is for you, and He is with you! This is a promise that will be our battle cry!

Remember, you are not your past mistakes or sins. The stains of your past are no longer visible, because the blood of Jesus has cleansed you. The past chapters of your life cannot be changed, but you can allow them to be testimonies of how far God has brought you. Your past is a witness that all things are possible through God. Your best days are ahead of you; just keep going. Keep fighting for who you are becoming. You were placed on this earth

> **The past chapters of your life cannot be changed, but you can allow them to be testimonies of how far God has brought you.**

at this specific time for an ordained purpose that only you can do. It is amazing to know that the God of all creation intentionally and uniquely created you for a purpose that only you can do. The storms of life may come, but our Savior calms them with the sound of His voice. You are a child of the Most-High God, and He will be with you in every battle you may find yourself in. So be encouraged, and be courageous. It's time to take back territory for the Kingdom of God!

Warrior's Prayer

Father in Heaven, hallowed be Your name, for You are sovereign over all creation. You who sit high in the Heavens above. God, you are the eternal Creator who has power and dominion over all creation. It is because of the sacrifice of Your one and only Son, Jesus Christ, that I can say in absolute faith that I am victorious! For the shed blood of Christ sealed the victory over my life by placing my faith in Him. I have faith that He lived, died, and rose again for my sins. I pray that You will equip me with Your armor to protect me from the fiery arrows of the enemy. I pray that You will give me a heightened sensitivity to Your voice and presence. I pray that You will give me heightened discernment, so that I may be vigilant against the deceitful tactics of the enemy. I surrender every battle that I am currently facing to You, Lord, who goes before me and fights for me. I place my hope, faith, trust, and confidence in You, Lord, for all areas of my life. I claim victory over the enemy through Jesus's finished work on the cross. It is the mighty matchless name of the resurrected king, Jesus Christ, I pray. Amen.

ACKNOWLEDGMENTS

First and foremost, I give all glory and praise to God. For without Him, and His Son, Jesus Christ, I would not be here today. I did not write a single word in this book without the guidance and direction of the Holy Spirit. This book is a true testament that if you believe in God, all things are possible in Him. I did not come this far in life without God or the people He placed in my path to help me along the way. I am a living testimony that God will finish all that He starts within you. I am a living testimony that all things are possible through

God and Him alone. Let our faith in Him be the fuel that guides us to Him.

To my wife, Sheryl: Sweet Pea, your constant support and sacrifice has not gone unnoticed. You have given up so much so that I may be in a position to be obedient to wherever God sends me. I thank you from the bottom of my heart. He designed you for me, and me for you. There is no doubt that I am who I am today because of you. I honor you, and I celebrate you for being the best part of me. Being your husband is one of the greatest honors of my life. I love you.

To my son, Christean: There is a reason and a purpose for why you are on this earth. I pray that your purpose will be fulfilled. I pray that all God has for you will, in His timing, come to pass. Put God first, and all things are possible that are in accordance with His will for your life. You are a blessing, and I have faith that you will do God's work that He has for you to accomplish.

To my grandmother Delores Ramey: Thank you for raising me, and for showing me a true example of what faithfulness to God is. It is because of your constant prayers that I am here today. I honor you, and I love you. I hope I will continue to make you proud.

To my grandfather Robert Ramey: Thank you also for raising me. I wish you could be here with us, but you are in a better place, in Heaven. Save a place for me. I cannot wait until we meet again. I love you.

To my mother, Mattie Mcfarland: Thank you for giving birth to me. I know it was not easy having a son at the age of twenty while being enrolled in college. You missed out on your college degrees because of me. This is why I chose to not only pursue my undergraduate degree but also my graduate degree. All of my accomplishments thus far have been fueled by your sacrifice. I love you.

To my bonus mother, Quendalyn: Thank you for always treating me as your own son. The kindness that you have shown me throughout the years is greatly appreciated. I will always remember it, and I am grateful to have you in my life.

To the men who were fathers in my life—Byron and Parnell: Thank you for filling this vacant spot in my life. I appreciate all of the wisdom and guidance you have given me throughout the years. I am the man I am today because you taught me to be so. I love you both, and I cannot thank God enough for all you have done for me.

To my beautiful aunts Priscilla and Rhonda: Thank you for being the best aunties I could possibly ask for. I pray that God will continue to bless you and keep you. I hope that I have made you proud—and that I will continue to do so.

To my beautiful aunt Sharon: May you rest in peace. Thank you for always being a person who loved family, and for always ensuring that I was moving in the right direction. You are, and will always be, greatly missed.

To my brothers Brandon, Darius, and Cyrus, and to my sisters Shankira and Miracle: Being your older brother has been one of the greatest honors of my life. I hope that my life has been a positive example for you all to follow. I look forward to all that the future holds for you.

To my cousins Adrianna, Ari, Quan, Devin, Kentrell, Marlowe, Marcus, and so many more to name: I pray that God will keep you and bless you. That in His will, you will have a blessed and prosperous life. I am proud of all of you, and I hope that you will love God as much as He loves you.

To my Delmundo family—Rex, Mama Jaquie, Richie, Rhianna, and our adopted Auntie Dhonna: Thank you for welcoming me into your family. Not only did I receive an amazing wife but I also received an amazing family. I am proud to be a part of your family, and I am grateful to have each of you in my life. I pray that God will continue to bless, protect, and watch over each one of you. You are all very special to me.

To my Covering, Apostle Loutricia Lee: God knew that I needed you on the path that He created me to walk. This book is not only a reflection of my obedience to Him but it reflects your obedience to Him as well. Because you said yes to Him, God led you to me, and I am extremely grateful to have you as a mentor on the path God created for me. Thank you for always praying for me, and for being there for me when I needed you most.

To Nik and Jay Griffin: Thank you for being a constant and consistent presence of encouragement in my life, and for allowing me to interrupt your many lunch breaks. Also, thank you for your constant fellowship, mentorship, and friendship. I pray that God will continue to bless, protect, and watch over you wherever He leads you.

To Marcus and Sariah: Thank for helping me with the ministry. One of my fondest memories during my time here in Italy will be your baptism, and surrendering your life to Christ! I know that God has amazing plans in store for you both. Continue to look to Him for guidance, and trust Him with all of your heart.

To Anna Krusinski: Thank you for helping me get my story to the world (again). God knew that I needed you, and I am confident that our meeting was ordained by Him. You are an amazing person, and a wonderful person to work with. God sees your humility, and He loves you very much. I pray that God will continue to bless you and keep you. Your humility and joy are contagious, and you are a light in this world. I am sure that we will work together again, and I am looking forward to that adventure.

To my biological father, Christopher Garner: You

may not have been present in my life, but you've had a purpose in it. If we never meet, I just want to say that I forgive you. I cannot blame you for things that are unknown to me. I didn't know your circumstances in life during the year of my birth, and I cannot selfishly hold that against you. I just want you to know that I am OK, and if you ever want to meet, I am here. I will not meet you with condemnation but with open arms, as a son welcomes his father. God bless you, and I pray that you find peace in this life, if we are never to meet.

ABOUT THE AUTHOR

CHRISTOPHER D. RAMEY was born and raised in Waynesboro, Mississippi. He is a lieutenant in the United States Navy where he has served on active duty for twelve years. He is fully committed to serving his Lord and Savior, Jesus Christ, which has led him to be the pastor of Redirection Ministries, a nondenominational military-based church service on US Naval Support Activity in Naples, Italy, where he currently resides with his wife, Sheryl Sullivan.